For my beautiful children,
Erin, Scott, Lani and Sam...

...because I love when you come home for lunch.

Contents

Introduction

Everyday around noon you are faced with the same question. "What's for lunch?" Are you filled with joy at the thought of yet another sandwich or making another box of macaroni and cheese? No?!? Then you've come to the right place.

Within these pages you will find a method of relief from the monotony and tedium of "what's for lunch." Relief from the health and $$ consequences of choosing fast food when you just can't face another sandwich or don't have time to prepare something more desirable.

Here also you will find dozens of really great choices to have for lunch, all that can be made in advance and frozen, ready for you to enjoy with very little time or effort spent in the kitchen.

Of course, you could keep your freezer stocked with prepackaged, frozen foods from the freezer section of the grocery store. They will cost you a bundle and you never know which ones you will like and which ones you will suffer through until they are gone, but they truly are convenient. Then again, you could create your own convenience. You could stock your freezer with a variety of lunches that *you* have prepared. You will have a delicious variety of options, be kinder to your health and your waistline, and save money, too.

Whether you are too busy to cook, you do not like to cook, or you are bored with repetitive lunch options, suffer no more. With **Lunch is Ready** as your guide, you can spend just one day cooking and fill your freezer with delicious lunches. Whether you freeze them in family-size or individual servings, they can be ready for you, hot and delicious in minutes.

Every aspect of the process is covered in this book. Everything from the equipment that will make your life easier to the more than 200 freezer-worthy lunch recipes to choose from. Chapter 11 is a sample outline with complete, step-by-step instructions to prepare a selection of lunches in one day. The recipes are listed and the order of events is outlined for you. Each recipe is delicious, family friendly and fairly simple. Following this example will guide you through a positive first experience. Each subsequent experience will be easier as you develop your own style and shortcuts.

No matter what your circumstances, having lunches in your freezer, making it possible for you to say "lunch is ready!" is a beautiful thing.

Chapter 1

Why Freeze?

Why freeze? Because you are busy! Your time is valuable. Freeze to create your own convenience - the convenience of enjoying lunch without a lot of fuss and effort. Freeze to create your own source of relief - the relief of enjoying a variety of lunches without a daily outpouring of time and creativity.

You can purchase plenty of convenience at the grocery store. Take a stroll down the freezer isle of your favorite grocery store. Notice the wide variety of frozen foods that can be purchased. Do these meet your expectations? Do you and your family enjoy them? Are they good for you? Can you afford them? When you freeze meals yourself, you have the advantage of freezing only those things your family enjoys, the way your family prefers them. Freeze what they like, what is good for them and what you can afford.

There are many reasons to freeze lunch recipes. Freeze because....

...you are ready for a change from having another boring sandwich for lunch. Freeze a variety of lunch favorites and truly enjoy lunchtime.

...sometimes your family is scattered at lunch time, leaving only one or two at home for lunch. Who wants to prepare an entire recipe and serve only one or two servings? You can prepare your favorite sandwich fillings, salad fillings and soups, freeze them in individual servings and be able to serve lunch for any number in a few minutes.

...sometimes everyone is home for lunch. Perhaps only on the weekends, but what a beautiful thing to be able to provide a wonderful lunch for the masses, and spend very little time in the kitchen. Frozen in family-sized portions, you can make your choice and have lunch ready in a few minutes. Frozen in individual servings, you can provide exactly the servings needed. No leftovers to deal with.

...you are not a short order cook! A variety of lunch choices in your freezer, frozen in individual servings, will allow you to accommodate everyone's lunch desires - if you desire to accommodate them, that is!

...you desire to have variety in the lunches that you or others carry to work. Frozen in microwave safe dishes, lunch can be taken to work frozen and heated in the microwave at lunch time. Imagine how easy to prepare each morning! Simply make your choice from the freezer and off you go!

...a thermos filled with warm BBQ beef or Sloppy Joes to put on a bun, or a thermos filled with hot soup is an exciting and welcome change from the same old peanut butter and jelly in the lunch box of your school aged children.

...you never again want to feel that "now what?" feeling that comes when you have unexpected guests at lunch time. Whether it be extra high school kids that come home for lunch with yours, or long lost friends from Kalamazoo, how wonderful to not feel the least bit of panic when inviting them to stay for lunch.

...some days you need lunch in a hurry, whether for one or for many. With lunches in your freezer you are always just a few minutes away from a delicious, satisfying lunch.

Chapter 2

What is Freezer-Worthy?

A recipe is considered freezer-worthy if it can be prepared, frozen, thawed, heated and served, and still be delicious and appealing to those who consume it. A general rule is that, if you see it frozen at the store you can probably freeze it successfully at home.

Most soup recipes can be successfully frozen. Prepare your favorite soup recipes. Allow them to cool and then package them for the freezer. Whether packaged in family-size or in individual bowls, soup makes a delicious lunch.

Cream based soups sometimes look lumpy after freezing but once you heat them up and stir, they usually look and taste delicious. Sometimes a recipe may thicken up a bit. Stir in a little milk, cream or broth until it is the consistency you prefer.

Potatoes in any recipe can be really fussy. Potatoes have a high moisture content and become mushy after freezing. Small pieces of potato in a soup or chowder that is meant to be cooked until the potatoes start to disintegrate can be frozen, but if you like nice firm chunks of potato in your soup, it probably shouldn't be frozen. You can substitute commercially frozen potatoes in some soup recipes. This type of potato has been flash frozen and the excess moisture removed so the potatoes don't turn mushy.

Most hot sandwich fillings freeze beautifully. From Sloppy Joes to BBQ Beef to Teriyaki Chicken, they all serve up as delicious as the day they were cooked. Freeze them in family-sized and individual portions.

Baked stuffed pocket sandwiches make wonderful quick lunches. They can be frozen before or after baking. If they are frozen before baking, it is easy to bake them on the day you want to serve them. Just pop a few in the oven or toaster oven until they are hot and toasty. If they are frozen baked and ready to eat, just thaw and heat. They can usually be thawed and heated in the microwave in a minute or two. Microwaving a baked stuffed sandwich will result in a soft crust. If you prefer the crust to be crispy, a minute or so under the broiler or in the toaster oven is all it will need to make it mostly crispy again.

You can freeze a wide variety of burger recipes. Preparing and freezing them will make it possible for you to serve truly delicious, unique burgers in no more time than to serve a regular burger. Burgers are best when frozen before cooking or grilling. However, freezing them already cooked or grilled provides the convenience of a speedy lunch. Be careful when reheating an already cooked burger, since overcooking tends to toughen ground meats. Experiment. Try both methods and see which you prefer.

Salads make a perfect lunch for some people. You can't freeze the entire salad but you can freeze the time con-suming part, such as the meat filling. How easy to have taco salad if you don't have to prepare the filling! Who wants to prepare an entire recipe of taco filling just to serve one taco salad for lunch? Prepare the salad fillings that you enjoy and freeze them in individual servings. Imagine the joy of your favorite salads for lunch without the daily hassle!

Pasta can be frozen successfully but it should be under-cooked. On the back of most pasta packages the recom-mended cooking time is listed. When you are cooking pasta to be frozen in a recipe, cook the pasta for two minutes less than the shortest recommended cooking time. For example, if you are cooking bow tie pasta and the back of the box suggests that you cook it for 9 to 11 minutes, cook it for only 7 minutes. Only add the pasta AFTER the water is boiling and set your timer as soon as you drop the pasta into the boiling water. You may think that the pasta could not possibly be done enough to add to your recipe, however, the pasta will continue to absorb moisture during the entire process of freezing, thawing and then heating. If you start with pasta that is fully cooked, it could get mushy. A timer becomes all the more important since overcooking the pasta can be disastrous and you won't even know it until you serve the meal later.

If you find that you dislike the texture of pasta that has been frozen, even when it is undercooked before freezing, you may want to prepare the recipe and exclude the pasta. On the day you serve the meal, cook the pasta and stir it in.

If you are uncertain if a recipe can be frozen successfully, freeze a small portion or even just a spoonful. The test for "freezer-worthiness" is, "Do you like it after it has been frozen?" After it is frozen, thawed and heated, can you tell that it has been frozen? If you can tell it has been frozen, you don't want it on your freezer-worthy list.

When you freeze food you are not sacrificing taste for convenience. You are not freezing leftovers. What makes leftovers taste like leftovers? Leftovers can taste dried out, thick and overcooked. Freezing is a marvelous method for food preservation. When frozen properly, the food you serve your family will taste as delicious as if made that day! The intention is to freeze food at or before its peak so you are always serving fresh tasting food.

Fully cooked meals such as Slow Cooker, StoveTop, Oven and Oven Assemble recipes should be frozen as soon as cool enough to go into the freezer. Assemble recipes should be frozen as soon as preparation and packaging is complete.

Although there are some guidelines concerning what may or may not be frozen, the freezer-worthy rule is a personal one. If you like it after it has been frozen, it is freezer-worthy. If you do not like it after it has been frozen, it does not make the freezer-worthy list. Simple as that.

Chapter 3

Things That Will Make Your Life Easier

The items listed and explained in this chapter are the same as the items listed in **Dinner is Ready**, with an additional two items at the end. Most of the items are used in the exact way they are used in **Dinner is Ready**, however some have additional convenient uses, not to be overlooked.

There is some basic equipment you should have in order to prepare many recipes in one day. The items listed in this chapter will make your life easier on Cooking Day. Most of these things you probably already have in your kitchen. For each item that you do not have, carefully consider its value and consider adding it to your collection.

Two Sets of Measuring Cups
Two sets of measuring cups are essential. More specifically, two different sets of measuring cups. One set for dry ingredients, one set for wet ingredients. If you only use one set of measuring cups, how much time will you waste washing out wet ingredients and then drying the measuring cup so you can measure something dry, only to have to measure something wet again? A set of measuring cups for wet ingredients and a separate set for dry ingredients is invaluable.

A set of "wet" measuring cups could include a set of nesting measuring cups with 1 cup, 1/2 cup, 1/3 cup and 1/4 cup measures, and a 2-cup glass liquid measure. A true liquid measure is one that when filled to capacity leaves room to move the cup without spilling the contents. Use this type to measure large quantities of liquid, such as water or chicken broth. This type of measure requires that you check the amount at eye level. Since there is certain amount of guessing involved to determine where "level" is, especially when measuring 1 cup or less, a set of nesting measuring cups is particularly helpful, even though they are not true liquid measures. When measuring ingredients of 1 cup or less, hold the measure over the bowl or very near to it, fill it to the brim and pour it in. There is no need to wash out the measuring cups unless flavors will collide, and even then usually a quick rinse is all it will need. There is no need to dry it out since a speck of water probably won't hurt any recipe you are preparing.

A set of "dry" measuring cups could be a different shape or color of nesting cups. If you purchase plastic measuring cups be sure to get the kind that the measurement numbers (1/4 cup, 1/3 cup, 1/2 cup, etc.) are in raised plastic. If they are just painted on, eventually the paint will come off and you will be left guessing which is the 1/4 cup and which is the 1/3 cup.

Use whatever combination of metal, plastic and/or glass measures that you are comfortable with. Just be sure you have a set for wet and a set for dry.

Two Sets of Measuring Spoons

You will need two different sets of measuring spoons for exactly the same reason you need two different sets of measuring cups. One set for wet, one set for dry. Keep things consistent and use the same type of measuring spoons and measuring cups to measure your dry ingredients and the same type of measuring spoons and measuring cups to measure your liquid or wet ingredients. In other words, if you use your metal set of measuring cups for wet ingredients, also use a metal set of measuring spoons for measuring liquid. If you choose plastic cups to measure dry ingredients, use plastic measuring spoons to measure dry.

As with the plastic measuring cups, if you purchase plastic measuring spoons, be sure the measurement number is in raised plastic, not stamped or painted on.

You might also consider getting a cute little glass measure for measuring up to 2 tablespoons at a time. It looks just like the larger 2 cup version in miniature. It has markings for 1 to 6 teaspoons, 1/2 to 2 tablespoons and 1/4 to 1 ounce measurements. It truly comes in handy when making double or triple recipes. This handy little item can be found at specialty kitchen stores and sometimes in the kitchen gadget section of grocery stores.

Canning Funnel

A canning funnel has a big opening at the bottom of the funnel. It is used for filling narrow mouth canning jars. The bowl of the funnel fits into a quart freezer bag. A serving spoon fits right through the mouth of the funnel. This makes for a marvelously easy, neat and tidy way to fill pint or quart freezer bags. Using a canning funnel ensures that you will not drip anything on the zipper part of the freezer bag while filling it. It is maddening to drip sauce on the zipper part of the bag then have to clean it off without spilling the contents and making a bigger mess. Save yourself the hassle and the cleanup time and get a canning funnel. You can usually get one anywhere you find canning supplies.

Large Mixing Bowls

Depending on your family size, you may be making double or even triple recipes. If this is the case, large mixing bowls come in really handy. Three or four is a good number. If you have several bowls, you can make several things at nearly the same time. Popcorn bowls are inexpensive, fairly easy to find and make perfect large mixing bowls. Nest them together and store them in the garage if you are short on cupboard space.

Large Pans
Making double or triple recipes of chili, spaghetti sauce, soup, etc. requires large pans. You can use your canner or any large capacity pan.

Large Mixing Spoons
You will need some fairly large spoons to mix your double batches. If the largest spoon in your drawer is the one you use to serve the peas, be kind to yourself and get some large spoons. However, for some cold recipes, especially meatloaf and meatball recipes, consider using your hands. It is faster, easier and more thorough than using a spoon.

Disposable Foil Baking Pans
You may not be using disposable foil baking pans as often to freeze lunches as you would to freeze dinners. However, if you have lunch recipes that you prefer to put in foil baking pans, choose the size that will be meals size for an individual or for your family. They come in every size, from very small to really large and every size in between. Small loaf pans are a good choice for packaging meals for one or two. Small cake pans are perfect for small families. You can get 8 x 8 square, 9" round, 9 x 13, and even larger.

They make for very easy cleanup, and are inexpensive enough to simply throw away. They can be reused if you wish, if you wash them out carefully. You can get these pans at most grocery stores. If not, ask the manager if they can get them for you. Most dollar stores and chain super stores carry them, too.

Extra Heavy Foil
You will need to cover the foil pans before you put them into the freezer. Use **Extra Heavy** foil. You will find it in the same place you get regular foil. It is much wider and heavier than regular foil. Read the box carefully before you

buy it. There is heavy duty foil that is slightly heavier than regular foil but it is not freezer foil. Be sure to get **Extra Heavy** foil. It will usually say "for freezing" somewhere on the box, usually on the back. It is the heaviest foil available to protect your food from freezer burn. Cut the foil about 1-inch larger than the pan and crimp this excess under the edges of the pan. There is no need to wrap the entire pan. Be careful with this stuff. The edges are stiff and very sharp.

Kitchen Scissors

A pair of kitchen scissors is a real time saver. Trimming or cutting up chicken, raw or cooked, is so much easier with scissors. Using scissors to cut some vegetables, such as green onions, makes the task easier. Cutting up bacon is a breeze with scissors. Seems you can never get that last strand of bacon with knife! You can cut a groove in the cutting board and still have that one skinny piece left! Use scissors! You will also need to cut your extra heavy foil to size depending on the size of the pan you are covering. Don't worry. Cutting foil is actually beneficial to the scissors. The foil helps sharpen your kitchen scissors as you cut.

Non-stick Cooking Spray

You may have many pans to grease. Spraying each pan with non-stick cooking spray will eliminate the time consuming and messy job of greasing each pan with shortening. It saves on calories, too.

Freezer Bags

Most dinners that you will put into the freezer can be stored in freezer bags. Good quality zipper freezer bags are wonderful. You can fill, press out the air, label, and layer them tidily in your freezer until you want them. Choose the size you need according to the size of your family and the size of the dinners you will be freezing. When filling a gallon bag, fold down the top few inches. This will protect the zipper from getting anything on it. It will also make the bag stable enough to stand up on its own, making it easier to fill. Use a canning funnel to fill quart or pint sized bags.

Disposable Plastic Storage Containers

These invaluable little beauties are wonderful. They come in many sizes and can be put in the freezer. These are especially perfect for freezing single servings of soup or other recipes. Choose the types that are easily re-usable, and are dishwasher, freezer and especially microwave safe.

Permanent Marker

Before each meal finds its way to the freezer, it will need to be labeled. Any medium point black permanent marker will do. If you use any other type of marker and it gets wet, you will be wondering what you are having for dinner. Each meal should be labeled with the name and the cooking instructions. You are busy! You don't have time to be looking up the cooking instructions when you want to serve a meal from your freezer. Write down everything you will need to know in order to serve the meal. Include the oven temperature, baking time, topping with crumbs or cheese, etc. You can either write directly on the bag, box or foil, or you can attach a label to each.

Food Processor

When it comes to chopping onions, anything that can make the task easier and quicker is a necessity. Use a food processor for uniform pieces of chopped onion. It also makes chopping bell peppers and other vegetables a breeze. You can chop or mince onion, mushrooms and even chicken in a fraction of the time that it would take to do the same job with a knife and cutting board. If your processor has a grating attachment you will love how easy it is to shred cheese, too.

Labels

If you choose to attach a label to each meal, you will need purchased labels. You can purchase sheets of labels to use with your computer or you could write on each. One benefit of using labels is you can make them the day before and just attach them as you go, rather than having to stop and write on each.

There is now a *30 Meals in One Day* computer program available. The *Lunch is Ready* version contains every recipe in this book and will allow you to enter any other recipes you desire. This program will adjust recipe sizes and print recipe cards. It will generate printable grocery shopping lists. It will print your chosen Menu complete with the date and the number of each meal you have frozen. It will print labels, ready to put on meals for the freezer, complete with recipe title and cooking/serving instructions. This program will streamline your efforts and is available in stores and at **www.dinnerisready.com**.

Timers

Even if you normally don't use a timer, you will want to get one or more. Your stove probably has one. Your microwave probably has one, too. If they don't, get one or more of the hand held kind. Having at least one additional timer makes it possible to time two things at the same time. You will need to time your pasta since it is imperative that it be undercooked. Even if you have a really reliable "internal clock," when cooking several things at the same time, you will find that it becomes increasingly more difficult to keep track of when each is done. Having multiple timers relieves your internal clock, eliminates the guesswork and helps prevent overcooking.

Rice Cooker

A rice cooker is certainly not a necessity, until you use one once. With a rice cooker you can cook a lot of rice to perfection every time. Turn it on, it times itself, turns off when the rice is done and you can dip into it each time you need rice. Clean up is a breeze. A rice cooker is certainly a beautiful thing!

Slow Cooker

A slow cooker is a marvelous cooking method that produces some of the yummiest of lunches with very little effort. A slow cooker provides even heat yet you don't have to watch it or stir it or ever worry about anything sticking or burning. Keep one or two working throughout the entire cooking day. Consider starting one working the night before cooking day, as well. Having one slow cooker is wonderful and, if you want to cook more than two slow cooker recipes in a day, having two slow cookers is a beautiful thing!

Multiple Trash Containers

Having many trash cans all around the kitchen will definitely make your life easier. In the course of making 15 recipes, how many things will you throw away? If you have to walk to the kitchen sink, open the cupboard door and lean over to toss away trash under the sink each time you throw something away, you will definitely waste a fair amount of time and effort. Place trash cans throughout your kitchen, not in your way, but wherever you will need them so that you don't have to take more than a step or two to toss anything away.

You don't need to purchase additional trash cans nor do you need to take trash cans from your bathrooms! Your trash cans do not have to be actual trash cans. Brown paper grocery bags make perfect temporary trash bags. Brown paper grocery bags are not too big and in the way, yet big enough to hold a fair amount. Easily attainable, too. When the bagger at the grocery store asks you "paper or plastic," just say "paper!"

Chapter 4

Choosing Recipes

Lunch doesn't have to be the same old thing everyday. Fill your freezer with a variety of lunch choices. If you already use the *30 Meals in One Day* process described in the book *Dinner is Ready*, this will be familiar territory for you. However, the outline and instructions are such that you don't need any prior instruction or experience. Preparing lunch recipes may be a smaller production than preparing dinner recipes, depending upon your family size, your need for lunches and the room you have available to store them in the freezer. Consider how many people are home for lunch. Perhaps it will be helpful for you to prepare meal-sized lunches. Perhaps having single servings in your freezer is all you really need or want. Perhaps a combination of the two options will be most convenient for you.

Chapter 15 of this book is a collection of freezer-worthy lunch recipes. They have all been freezer tested. Chapter 11 is sample outline for preparing 10 lunch recipes in one day. You could use the outline exactly for a guided first experience. You could, of course, make your own selections based on your needs. Decide how many different lunch options you desire to have ready in your freezer. No matter how many recipes you choose, even if you only choose a few recipes, be sure to choose recipes from different categories so you can prepare several recipes at the same time, rather than preparing one recipe at a time.

When preparing lunches for the freezer, double or even triple each recipe. It takes virtually no more effort to make a double batch of almost any recipe. This is especially true with soups and sandwich fillings. An exception would be making recipes such as the filled pocket sandwiches. Of course, the more of this type of recipe you prepare, the longer it will take. However, once you have the filling made and have set up the ingredients, the process will take a shorter period of time to make many all at once than it will to make a few on two or more occasions.

It is important that you freeze meal-size, not recipe size. If you are cooking for one or for two or for a small family, perhaps a recipe will already make two meals. You won't need to adjust the recipe. You could cut the recipe down, but why? It takes no less time to make half a recipe. Make the entire recipe and divide into meal-sized portions. If it makes more than two meals, consider this a bonus! If you are cooking for 4 and the recipe is for 6, you will need to increase the recipe by half. If you are cooking for 6 and the recipe is for 6, you will need to double the recipe. Whatever your family size, adjust each recipe so that it makes at least two meals.

Don't be too concerned about having to eat the same thing for lunch. Most of these recipes will easily keep for at least two months, many of them will keep for up to six months in the freezer. There are so many freezable soups, salads and sandwich fillings to choose from! Choose different recipes each time. Plus, by overlapping your cooking days you will increase the variety of meals you have to choose from.

The **30 Meals in One Day** computer program allows you to easily **adjust recipe sizes**, as well as many other time saving functions. Please refer to the box on page 15 for more information.

Recipe Cards

Whether you use recipes from this book, from your own collection or a combination of both, you will want to put each recipe on a separate 4 x 6 card. I know, I know. You have your favorite recipe collection and you like it just the way it is, thank you very much. Perhaps it is all neatly bound in the notebook grandma gave you, or perhaps it is in 14 different cookbooks but you are so familiar with them you can flip right to them whenever you want. Maybe you are completely comfortable with that cardboard box of miscellaneous recipes that you dig through each time you need a recipe.

Each of those methods has its benefits, but when you are preparing a few lunch recipes on the same day you do not want to be flipping back and forth in books or binders or digging in your beloved box. Your cooking day will not only be easier but will be more rewarding if you have a separate recipe card for each recipe you prepare. It will be easier because you will need recipes near the crock pot, recipes near the stove, and recipes on the counter. As the dishes are prepared and moved to the table to cool, the recipe card follows, so you can refer to it when you label the package for the freezer. It will be rewarding because as you finish a recipe and it has cooled, been packaged, and labeled you get to put that recipe into the beautiful DONE pile. Oh, the satisfaction of watching that pile grow!

Save guesswork in the future by writing how many meals your version of the recipe will make, directly on the recipe card. Mark on each card the number of freezer bags or containers you will need in order to package the number of meals that recipe will make. It is also helpful to write on the top, right corner of the recipe card, the type of cooking method required for the recipe: Slow Cooker, Oven, StoveTop, Oven Assemble or Assemble.

The *30 Meals in One Day* computer program will **print recipes** and save you a bucket of time. Print and use the recipes you need, then either file them away or toss them! You can print a new selection of recipes next time if you desire. See page 15 for more information.

Fully Cooked is generally anything that you would normally cook completely on the stove top or slow cooker and put on the table.   Some examples of *Fully Cooked* recipes are soups and sandwich fillings.   These recipes you will cook completely, allow to cool and package them for your freezer. To serve, you will thaw them, heat to piping hot and serve.

Assembled and Ready to Bake or Cook includes such recipes as pocket sandwiches, burgers and pizza. These recipes you will prepare just to the point of baking or cooking, then you will package them for the freezer. To serve, you will thaw them, then bake or cook, and serve.

Cooking Methods

Before choosing your recipes you must first divide them according to cooking method and/or time required to prepare each.   Slow Cooker recipes, Oven recipes, StoveTop recipes, Oven Assemble recipes and Assemble recipes.

Your recipe list should very nearly consist of:
- 1 Slow Cooker recipe
- 1 Oven recipe
- 2 StoveTop recipes
- 2 Oven Assemble recipes
- 4 Assemble recipes

Of course, the number of each type of recipe that you choose could possibly vary at times. Just be sure to choose recipes carefully and realistically. Avoid choosing too many labor intensive recipes.

Choose 1 Slow Cooker recipe

The number of Slow Cooker recipes you can choose depends

on the number of slow cookers you have and the time required for each recipe.

Generally, Slow Cooker recipes can be cooked on High for 4 to 6 hours or on Low for 8 to 10 hours. This is not a rule, just a guideline. If you desire to cook two recipes in one day and both recipes give you the option of cooking on High for 4 to 6 hours or less, you can probably accomplish this. Choose only one recipe if your recipe requires 8 to 10 hours and you have only one slow cooker.

If you have the opportunity to do some preparation the day before your cooking day, consider starting a recipe in the slow cooker before you go to bed. Choose a recipe with a Low 8 to 10 hours or longer cooking time. By the time you get up in the morning you'll already have one recipe cooked and ready to be cooled and packaged for the freezer. You can immediately start a new recipe in the slow cooker.

It is feasible that you could cook four Slow Cooker recipes with only one slow cooker if you choose two Low 8 to 10 hour recipes and two High 4 to 6 hour or less recipes. Cook one of the Low 8 to 10 hour recipes the night before cooking day. First thing on cooking day replace that recipe with a High 4 to 6 hour recipe. When it is done, immediately replace it with another short cooking recipe. Then before you go to bed at night, put the last of the four recipes, a long cooking recipe, in the slow cooker.

Choose 1 Oven recipe
Oven recipes are cooked in the oven before freezing. These recipes can require lengthy baking times. They can also be those recipes that you desire to bake prior to freezing to provide you with the convenience of thawing a completely cooked meal that can be quickly heated and served. Bake these on cooking day, cool, and freeze. To serve, you will

simply thaw, heat and enjoy! You could bake more than one Oven recipe but consider that you may also be preparing Oven Assemble recipes. These recipes will require space in the oven even if only briefly. You can bake both types of recipes if the oven temperature requirements are not too drastically different.

Choose 2 StoveTop recipes

StoveTop recipes include those recipes that are prepared on a burner on the stove top. These recipes tend to be time consuming and labor intensive so you won't want to include too many. Most stoves have four burners. You do not want more than two burners occupied with recipes since you will need the other burners for other cooking needs such as browning, etc. If you choose more than two StoveTop recipes, be sure to choose simpler ones. Limit yourself to only two labor intensive StoveTop recipes. Remember to double or even triple the recipe. You might even consider making as much as the pot will hold.

Choose 2 Oven Assemble recipes

These are recipes that you assemble and bake for a brief period of time. Most take only a few minutes of baking time. They are then allowed to cool and are packaged for the freezer. To serve, you will thaw, then heat in the microwave or toaster oven. Some can even be heated straight from the freezer. If they will soften up in the microwave you can usually make them crisp again by placing them under the broiler in your oven or placing them in a toaster oven for a minute or two.

Choose 4 Assemble recipes

Assemble recipes require very little or sometimes no cooking before they are frozen. These recipes will be frozen prior to heating or baking. They are the least time consuming, the most rewarding and are just as tasty as the others.

Chapter 5

Lists That Will Make Your Life Easier

List Chosen Recipes

As you choose your recipes, make a list of the recipe titles. This list will become your *Menu* and will help you remember what you have in your freezer. Write down how many of each recipe you put in the freezer, or put a square or circle in front of the name for each meal you freeze. Keep track of the number of single servings as well as meal-sized containers you place in the freezer. If you place freezer bags filled with frozen portions of sandwich fillings, record these on your list. As you take a meal from your freezer, mark off the circle or square. This way you will always know what is in your freezer.

You could date each meal that you place in the freezer. I will not discourage you from doing so, however, I will say that I have *not* found that dating the meals in my freezer has been particularly helpful. When I forget about something in the freezer and then I find it later at the bottom of my freezer and the date tells me it is a year old I think, "Yep, it's a year old."

What DOES help me is dating the list. With a date at the top of the list, you can always tell what is in your freezer and how long it has been there. Add to the list as you add other things to your freezer. Always add the correct date.

The **30 Meals in One Day** computer program will make this list for you. It will print out your List of Chosen Recipes or **Menu**, complete with the number of each meal you freeze and date that you put it in the freezer. See page 15 for more information.

Following is a sample list as you can make for yourself or print from the computer program:

TODAY'S DATE

☐☐☐	Zesty Beef and Vegetable Soup
☐☐	BBQ Pork Sandwiches
☐☐☐☐	Teriyaki Chicken Bowls
☐☐	Chili CheeseSoup
☐☐	Pizza Roll-Ups
☐☐	Chicken Squares
☐☐☐	Honey Mustard Turkey Burgers
☐☐☐☐	BBQ Chicken Mini Pizzas
☐☐	Italian Heroes
☐☐	Beef Taco Filling

As a meal is removed from the freezer, be sure to check the corresponding box off the list. This way you will always know what you have in the freezer and you will be able to tell at a glance how soon you need to replenish your supply of frozen meals.

This list actually has two purposes. The first, of course, is to help you keep track of what is in the freezer. The second is it becomes your *menu* of sorts. Do you ever feel frustrated about the question, "What's for lunch?" This list will make answering this question easier for you. Simply choose a meal from the list.

Post this list in a convenient, easily accessible place. Post it on the inside of a cupboard door, on the refrigerator door or on the freezer door. The list is only helpful if it is kept up to date. If it is lost in a drawer somewhere it will probably not get updated as you add to and take away from the freezer. If it gets used to hold your place in the phonebook, becomes Algebra homework scratch paper or gets thrown away with a pile of newspaper, the list becomes completely useless!

Shopping List
Making a shopping list is an absolute must. If you are one who wouldn't dream of shopping without a list you will be comfortable with this. If you are one who likes to go to the store and "wing it," well, don't. You are sure to miss some little thing that will either prevent you from preparing the recipe you started, or cause you to interrupt your momentum to run to the store to retrieve the required item. In the long run, a list saves you time and frustration.

Start with your 10 recipes in front you. You will also need a pencil and a sheet of notebook paper or something similar in size. Forget the skinny little shopping list paper. You need to be able to *see* everything you are shopping for.

Group the items on your list by category. For example, list all the meat on the first lines on the left side of the page. Make hash marks as you go. One hash mark for each chicken breast or pound of chicken, one hash mark for each pound of ground beef, one hash mark for each pork chop, and one hash mark for each pound of spare ribs. Next group all dairy products. Use one hash mark for each cup of milk, sour cream and so on. Group all canned goods. Use one hash mark for each can. Be sure to write down the number of ounces, if it is an unusual amount or if it is a can of something that comes in multiple sizes. Group all frozen foods.

Use one hash mark for each box, can or bag, noting the ounces or size when necessary. Group all pasta. Use one hash mark for each type and size bag or box of pasta. Group all fresh produce. Keep track of vegetables by the piece or by the pound. For example, use one hash mark for each onion and one hash mark for each pound of baby carrots.

Group all packaging materials, and any other categories you need. Once you fill up one side of the paper with groups, make a second column of groups on the right hand side of the same side of the paper. Continue to add ingredients to the list as you go through each recipe card.

The *30 Meals in One Day* computer program will make this process simple. As you choose your recipes, the computer program simultaneously generates your **Shopping List**. When you are finished choosing recipes, your shopping list can be printed out, already in categories, and you are ready to head to the store!

Shopping from a list that is divided into categories will help prevent you from overlooking needed items. As you come to each department of the grocery store you will be able to get everything on the list in that particular category. It is more likely that you will be to the end of the list by the time you get to the end of the store! How frustrating it is to realize that you have overlooked a few things and now have to go back through the store to find them.

If you already have an item in your kitchen, there is no need to add it to your grocery list. Just be sure you do not "use" the same item from your cupboard in more than one recipe. For example, if you need soy sauce for 4 recipes, make sure that the amount of soy sauce you do have will be sufficient for all four recipes.

You will be packaging your lunches in freezer pans, freezer

bags, and plastic freezer containers. Decide which method you prefer for each recipe and count how many disposable foil baking pans, freezer bags, and plastic freezer containers you will need. Don't forget the extra heavy foil.

Following is a sample of a shopping list you could make for yourself or print from the computer program.

SHOPPING LIST

Meat
ground beef //
chicken breast ### /
stew meat /
pork tenderloin /

Produce
cabbage /
celery /
carrots //
onions ###

Dairy
Mozzarella ///
cream cheese /

Frozen
frozen bread dough /
green beans (15-oz) //

Bakery/Breads
English muffins ### /
French bread /

Canned Goods
spicy tomato juice (48-oz) /
chicken broth (14.5-oz) //
green chiles (4-oz) ///

Other
seasoned croutons

Seasonings
Italian seasoning
taco seasoning //

Packaging
plastic freezer containers
gallon freezer bags

Worcestershire sauce
vinegar

After you have made your shopping list, arrange your recipes in the order you will be preparing them. Arrange the cards with the Slow Cooker recipes first, then Oven, then StoveTop, then Oven Assemble and then the Assemble recipes. Arrange the Slow Cooker recipes with the shortest cooking time recipe first.

Arrange the remainder of the recipes in order starting with the one that takes the longest and ending with the easiest one. It can be discouraging to get to the end of the cooking day and find that you have a complicated recipe still to make. Prepare the hardest recipes or the recipes you least enjoy making first. When you complete recipe number 9 and you find that number 10 is an easy recipe or one you truly enjoy making you will be so glad you took a minute to put your recipes in order before starting!

Chapter 6

The Day Before

Shop

Your recipes are chosen and your list is made. You're ready to shop. Try to shop the day before you cook rather than the day you plan to cook. You do not want to begin your cooking day with a huge shopping excursion. Shopping can wear a person out and you will want to start out fresh. So, DO NOT shop on cooking day, but do try to shop the day before.

There are plenty of things you can do after you shop to prepare for cooking day. Your preparations will make your cooking day go smoothly. Before you leave for the store, clear everything off your counters and table that you will not need on the day you cook, and then go shopping.

Arrange the Goods

When you get home do NOT put everything away. There is no reason to find room in your cupboards for all the goods since you will be using them tomorrow on cooking day. Refrigerate anything perishable but leave the rest out. Stack all the canned goods near the can opener. Anything you know you will be using at the stove put them near the stove. Any ingredients that you will be mixing or assembling at the counter, arrange them to the side of the counter. There will be plenty of things that you already have in your cupboards that you will also need, such as salt, vinegar, soy sauce, etc. Get these things out so they will be handy and available the second you need them. Retrieve all those goods from your food storage that you didn't have to buy because you already have plenty. Go shopping in your own pantry. You don't want to make 47 trips to your food storage, wherever it may be. Arrange everything neatly on the counter with the labels turned so that you can easily identify each.

After you empty the bags of groceries, don't fold up the bags. Put one brown paper grocery bag near the can opener, one beside the counter, one near the stove, one near the table, and anywhere else you will be working. The idea is to make sure you have the capability of throwing anything away without having to take more than a step or two. This will keep your work space tidier and easier to work in and it will save you steps. When you are cooking all day, any step you can save is a plus. Grocery bags work splendidly since they are large enough to contain a fair amount of trash, yet they are narrow enough to be set on the floor next to counter (or wherever) and not be tripped over.

Choose a place that you will package your lunches for the freezer, such as the kitchen table. This is the spot to place all your freezer bags, boxes and pans. Put the foil and your marker and/or labels on the table. Also put the non-stick cooking spray and some trivets on the table. After you make a recipe and it needs to cool, you can set it on a trivet on the table to cool. When it is cool, everything you need to package, label, and freeze it will be readily accessible.

Chop the Vegetables

After you come home from shopping and have arranged the goods, you may want to make some further preparations for cooking day. If you have the time and the desire, chop the vegetables. Count how many onions you need diced, and dice them up. Use your food processor if you have one. Place them into a bag or a bowl, cover, and refrigerate. You can take care of any other vegetable preparation your recipes call for. Peel and slice the carrots, slice the onions, dice the bell peppers, slice the mushrooms, etc. You will probably need more chopped onions than any other veg- etable. Even if you only chop your onions the day before, it will be a huge help to you on cooking day. A big bowl of chopped onions on cooking day is a beautiful thing!

Shred the Cheese
Count the number of cups of cheese that need to be shred- ded. Use your food processor if you have one. If you do not you will definitely want to shred your cheese the day before you cook. Put the shredded cheese into a bowl or reseal- able plastic bags and place in the refrigerator until needed. Sometimes shredded cheese at the grocery store is the same price or only slightly more than a block of cheese. In this case, you may want to buy the shredded. The time saved is valuable. You may want to buy the cheese already shredded no matter how much extra the cost. Whatever method you choose and are comfortable with, shredded cheese on cooking day is a beautiful thing.

Cook the Chicken
Refrigerate all the meat except the chicken. Separate all the recipes that call for cooked chicken and count the amount of chicken required. It is a close guess to say that 1 chicken breast equals 1 cup of cooked chicken. Of course, chicken breast sizes vary but as an average this is a good rule of thumb. Put the counted pieces of chicken in a big pot with a piece of celery broken in half, a large washed but unpeeled carrot with the ends removed and broken in half, and a large peeled and quartered onion. Cover all ingredi- ents with water, add a few peppercorns and some salt, and cook the chicken until it is done. Remove the chicken to cool.

While the chicken is cooling, either strain the broth or just remove and discard the cooked vegetables and pepper-corns. SAVE THE BROTH. You can use it tomorrow in any recipe that calls for chicken broth. If there is still broth remaining you can add some more chopped vegetables and noodles to make a fabulous chicken soup. Why pay for canned chicken broth when you can make tastier broth just from cooking the chicken you need cooked anyway.

When the chicken is cool enough to work with, either chop with scissors or shred it into a large bowl(s). Cover the bowl and refrigerate this till tomorrow when you cook. A big bowl of cooked and chopped or shredded chicken on cook-ing day is a beautiful thing.

Thaw all the Meat
Perhaps you have meat in your freezer you will be cooking on cooking day. Be sure to get it out of the freezer in time to thaw for cooking day. Thaw all meat in the refrigerator. You can thaw and refreeze meat without consequence if the meat is never allowed to come to room temperature. Meat that is allowed to come to room temperature can allow harmful bacteria to grow which can cause illness. Always thaw meat in the refrigerator.

While certainly not mandatory, all the advanced prepara-tion you do will make your cooking day much easier. Waking up on the day you are going to put lunches in your freezer, with these preparations already accomplished, is truly a beautiful thing.

Chapter 7

Cooking Day

Preparing lunch recipes and freezing them for your convenience in the future is probably not going to be as big a production as putting 30 dinners in your freezer. You may not be making as much or as many. Then again, you may desire to have more lunch recipes than dinner recipes in your freezer. Either way, being organized and prepared on cooking day will make the entire process easier and more efficient.

Perhaps the most important preparation you can make for cooking day is to arrange your day. Choose a day that you have no obligations that will interrupt you and take you away from the kitchen. Eliminate the need to run errands, have someone else drive car pool, arrange for someone to help you with the children, don't answer the phone! (okay, except for emergencies). Combine children and cook with a friend, or trade cooking and tending days. Cook one day while she tends your children and then you can tend her children on another day while she cooks.

Sometimes you will not be able to complete all, or perhaps any, of the food preparation the day before. If this is the case, the Chapter 6 preparations are what you will do first. Clear every unnecessary thing off the counters and table. Set out the brown paper grocery bag trash containers. Start your slow cooker. You'll want to get every working moment you can from your slow cooker. Cook, cool and chop or shred the chicken. Chop the vegetables, especially all the onions. Shred all the cheese you will need. You don't want to have to stop to peel and chop an onion, or shred cheese, or cook, cool and shred chicken each time you need some. Stopping to perform these tasks over and over during your cooking day is a time waster, a momentum breaker, a motivation killer! Do these tasks once and be finished with them.

Your slow cooker is already working. Now fill the oven. Put both recipes in the oven if they will fit at the same time. If not, start with the recipe with the shortest cooking time. Next start the StoveTop recipes. Don't make both StoveTop recipes at the same time. They are time consuming and labor intensive. Just babysit one recipe at a time. While the StoveTop recipe is cooking you can begin assembling recipes at the counter. Remember to keep an eye on the stove top. Keep a running list of what is cooking and the times they are done or need an ingredient added. If the slow cooker is done in 3 hours, write down "Slow Cooker" or the recipe title. Next to that, write what time it will be in 3 hours, say 11:30. Be sure to write the time the recipe is done! If you simply write 3 hours, you are sure to wonder what time you started.

When you have the slow cooker working, the oven working and a recipe started on the stove top, you'll be ready to begin assembling recipes. Arrange the chosen Assemble recipes in the order you plan to make them. Start with the most difficult recipe or the one you least enjoy making. End with the easiest recipe or the recipe you enjoy making the most. Don't succumb to thinking that you should break yourself in gently on cooking day by making the easiest recipes first! If you put off making the most difficult recipe until the end...after you've prepared 9 other recipes...how likely will you be to actually make that difficult recipe? Be kind to yourself and prepare the difficult recipe first while you are fresh. The easy recipe is your final recipe, sort of your reward. You finish the easy one and you're finished!

Before you start assembling the first recipe, look ahead to the second. Does it call for something that can be cooking while you assemble number one? If so, start cooking the pasta, rice, etc. Use a timer so you don't have to remember when it is done. While it is cooking, assemble the first recipe. You may be finished assembling it before the pasta for recipe number two is done. If not, the timer will tell you when the pasta is done. You can drain it and it can sit in the sink and wait for you while you finish the first recipe. When finished with the first, move on to the second. The pasta is ready to go and all you need to do is assemble the ingredients, but before you begin to assemble it look ahead to the third. If it needs something that you can start while making the second, start it. This way you stay one recipe ahead of the assembly process and are always ready to move on to the next.

Prepare the Oven Assemble recipes while the Oven recipes are baking. Once the Oven recipes are done, your oven will already be hot and ready to bake the Oven Assemble recipes.

As recipes are done, move them to the table to be packaged for the freezer. The recipe card travels along with the food so that you can refer to it for any cooking instructions you want to include on the label.

Once your meals are labeled they are ready to be frozen. Put the recipe card in the *done* pile. When the StoveTop and Oven recipes are done you can move them to the table on trivets to cool. Recipe cards travel right along with them. If you have other recipes for the stove top or oven, start them. If not, continue to assemble recipes at the counter, cooking pasta, etc. as you go. When the meals cooling on the table are cool, put meal-sized portions into freezer containers or freezer bags and label.

In Chapter 11, a sample 10-recipe cooking day is complete-ly mapped out for you, step by step. If all 10 recipes appeal to you, start with this. Or substitute recipes with similar cooking requirements for the recipes that don't appeal to you and stick closely to the outline.

There is no disguising the fact that preparing 10 different recipes in one day requires your undivided attention for a significant amount of the day. It is not overly difficult but it will require a few hours to accomplish. However, it is important to remember that the time and effort you spend today will result in one day of freedom for each meal you place in the freezer. Also important to note is that prepar-ing many meals in one day will consume much less time than preparing the same number of meals individually.

After you have accomplished preparing many meals in one day, your subsequent experiences will flow more smoothly and will be less time consuming. You will settle into your own method and discover your own shortcuts.

I have cooked with many different people. Some I knew before our cooking experience and some I did not know before I helped them cook. Based on my experience, I have found that there are two main types of cooks. I affection-ately call them the Chaos Queens and the Neat Freaks.

The Chaos Queens are comfortable in their chaos. The Chaos Queens like to leave the groceries in the grocery bags and retrieve just what they want when they need it. This defeats the whole save-every-unnecessary-step theory. If you have to go to the grocery bag and then to the can open-er each time you need a can of soup, you have wasted a lot of effort and time in the course of a cooking day. Throwing away boxes or wrappers immediately is okay with the Chaos Queen, but it's also okay with them if they get thrown away later. They may have two sets of measuring spoons and cups, but part of one set is probably in the dishwasher or in the toy box. This is okay with them. They get over it as they go. A little time lost here because they had to rinse and dry out the measuring cup so they can measure ingredients is tolerated. Tolerated but not helpful.

Chaos is okay on a meal-by-meal basis but it really doesn't work when you are cooking many meals in just one day. You must be somewhat organized. You will become frustrated and lose your momentum if you have to stop and search for the measuring cups, or the vinegar, or the soy sauce each time you need it.

The Neat Freaks are completely uncomfortable with anything out of order. I have noticed that Neat Freaks have the most difficulty adapting to the multiple meals in one day effort. They feel the need to wash, dry and put away every spoon, bowl and measuring cup as well as put away every salt shaker and bottle of soy sauce as it is used.

Many times, while cooking with a neat freak, I have set down a measuring cup and when I reached for the same one 3 minutes later, it was gone. I would look around for it and find it either in the dishwasher or back in the drawer! Choose something that you use a lot, let's say the salt. Now let's say you will be using the salt 12 times on cooking day. You can demonstrate the loss of time. Walk to the cupboard and get out the salt, walk to the counter to add it to a recipe, then walk back to cupboard and put it away. Repeat this 12 times and you will see what a lot of wasted effort is involved in putting everything away each time!

Neat Freaks also have a hard time using the same bowl to mix up one recipe after another was made in it. They feel it must be washed, rinsed, dried and put away before it can be used again. If you feel this way, let me say this gently. It is okay to rinse and reuse a bowl that has been used to mix another recipe in it first. It does not have cooties. Nothing has been in it long enough to spoil or be dirty in any way. Of course, the exception is that anything that has touched raw meat must be washed with soap and hot water immediately.

If you are a Neat Freak you must "let your hair down" just one day. Let things stay out until their use is over for just one day. All 29 other days of the month you can have complete order in your kitchen. If you are a Chaos Queen, "put your hair up" just one day and be better organized. It will save you time and you will not regret it.

Whether you are a Chaos Queen, or a Neat Freak, or somewhere in the middle, seek to have organized chaos in your kitchen on cooking day. Things may appear chaotic but don't let them get sloppy. Keep things out that you need, put them away when they've been used for the last time, wash a little as you go, take out and replace trash bags as they fill. Don't succumb to interruptions. You will be much happier and your experience will go much more smoothly and pleasantly.

Chapter 8

Packaging for the Freezer

Your freezer packaging options are many. They include reusable plastic freezer containers, resealable freezer bags, and disposable aluminum pans. Each of these comes in a wide variety of sizes. Using containers designed for the freezer ensures that your meals will come out of the freezer as tasty as they went in.

Any food that is exposed to the air is subject to freezer burn. As food freezes, the air draws the moisture out. Notice any frost on your food? This is freezer burn. The moisture has been drawn out by the air and forms ice crystals. Chicken and other meats turn white and rubbery. Pasta gets dry, white and eventually crumbles. This is freezer burn. It can be prevented by eliminating as much air as possible from your packaged dinners.

Manufacturers are continually coming out with new and better products for freezing and storing food. Keep an eye out for new products that will improve your life and make your meal preparation and freezing easier.

Reusable Plastic Freezer Containers
Plastic freezer containers come in many sizes and can be used many times. Be sure to purchase only the type that are labeled freezer, microwave and dishwasher safe. Being able to microwave meals is a huge time saver when you have very limited time to serve a meal.

Plastic freezer containers are especially handy for soup since the rigid sides of the container provide more stability. You can write the name of the recipe and any cooking instructions right on the lid or you can attach a label. If you use a permanent marker to label the lid, any scouring powder will easily remove the ink and you will be able to re-label it each time it is used. Labels are easily soaked off.

When you use this type of container, leave 1/4-inch head-space so the food has room to expand as it freezes. Otherwise, the food will expand and pop the lid off in the freezer. Air causes freezer burn so try to never let chicken or other meat be exposed to the air, even within a freezer container. If the container has room left after you have placed the desired amount of food in the container, press a piece of plastic wrap onto the surface of the food and replace the lid. This will help protect the food from the air and subsequent freezer burn.

This type of container is especially useful for freezing single servings. Having an assortment of single servings will make lunch easy and enjoyable. They make a welcome change from another boring sandwich for lunch. They are easy to take from the freezer in the morning for you or others in your life who carry lunch to work. They are also handy for days when the family is scattered and only one or two are home at lunchtime.

Resealable Freezer Bags

There are quite a few brands of resealable freezer bags. Be sure to get good quality freezer bags with good thick plastic and solid seams. Some of the lower quality bags tend to break at the seams and sometimes the zipper doesn't line up. Buy the best brand that you can that is on sale. Seems there is always one on sale.

Whether you write on the bag with a permanent marker or attach a label, label your freezer bag before you put the food into it. The food, especially anything cold, tends to make the bag sweat. It is difficult to write on anything wet, even with the best of permanent markers.   Labels don't cooperate under moist conditions either.

When you are ready to put a meal into a gallon size freezer bag, open the bag and fold the top couple of inches of the bag back over itself. This will give the bag stability, making it easy to fill. The bag will stand up and stay open by itself. Hold on to one side as you fill the bag so that it doesn't fall over when full of food. Folding the bag back will also make it easier to protect the zipper of the bag. This prevents the tedious and messy job of cleaning any drips off the zipper so that it will seal properly.

To fill a quart or pint size freezer bag, use your canning funnel. You will find that a standard canning funnel, the size used for narrow mouth canning jars, fits perfectly in the top of a quart or pint-sized bag. You can hold the top of the bag right around the bowl of the funnel and filling the bag is a breeze. A standard size serving spoon fits nicely into the mouth of the funnel if you are using a spoon.

Whichever size of freezer bag you use, be sure to press all the air out of the bag before you seal it. This is a very important step since air causes freezer burn. Any air left in the bag dries out the food during storage. The moisture is drawn out of the food and forms a frost in the package. If all the air is pressed out and the bag is touching the food, freezer burn can be prevented. Fold any unused portion of the bag under the food and make a flat, stackable package.

If you are unsure about the amount of a recipe like soup to put into a freezer bag, measure each family member's portion. You can give a pretty close guess to how much each family member eats. You've been feeding them for how long?! Place the soup, into a serving bowl to represent one family member's portion. Then measure the food with a measuring cup. Write down the amount. Do this for each member of the family. Some may eat an entire bowl full, others may eat half a bowl. If members of your family normally want seconds or thirds, add this to the total. Also factor in your desire for leftovers and perhaps the likelihood of a guest at mealtime. Write the total right on your recipe card. You'll never again wonder how much you should measure into a freezer bag for a family sized meal. You could also determine the total amount that will go into the freezer bag using water, if you don't want to measure actual food.

If, after serving a recipe, you notice that you had way too much or not quite enough, be sure to adjust your notes on your recipe card so that it will be near perfect next time.

Disposable Foil Pans

Disposable foil pans come in about any size you desire - single servings all the way to large pot luck size and every size in between. Some even come with neat and tidy foil-lined tops that you lay on top of the pan and then crimp the edges over. Don't be concerned about the shape of the pan, rather choose the pans that will contain the number of servings you need for one meal.

After filling the pan with food, either attach the foil-lined top, or cover it tightly with extra heavy foil. It is not necessary to wrap the pan entirely, just cover the top and crimp over the edges. Press the foil right down on top of the food to eliminate as much air as possible. Remember, air is not your friend in the freezer. Write the name of the recipe and any cooking instructions right on the foil or foil-lined cover. Labels attach easily if you prefer them.

Chapter 9

The Freezer

Most lunches you place in your freezer will remain delicious for a few weeks and some recipes will last for up to six months if packaged properly and if your freezer is maintained at zero degrees or lower. Food items such as pizzas and baked pocket sandwiches should be used within a few weeks. They are difficult to wrap airtight and are more subject to freezer burn and drying out. Other recipes that can be frozen in freezer bags or containers will last for up to about six months.

It is important that each meal be cooled completely before putting it into the freezer. Putting many recipes of warm food into your freezer can cause the temperature to rise within the freezer and the quality of the food you already have in the freezer could be compromised. Also, the freezer motor could be overworked and could be damaged. If you have only a small freezer in your refrigerator, you may even want to put some of your packaged meals into the refrigerator and allow them to be completely cold before adding them to the freezer.

If you have only a small freezer in your refrigerator, your challenge to fit many meals is greater. You will need to stack your meals carefully, and take advantage of every available space in your freezer. You may need to have only one box of ice cream at a time in your freezer for a couple of weeks until half of the meals are gone.

The space in a refrigerator freezer is deceptive. You really can get a lot more into a refrigerator freezer than it appears you can. Also, remember that you are freezing meal-size not recipe-size and that you are not freezing bulky pans or dishes. Food in a plastic bag takes up a lot less space than the same food in a baking or serving dish.

Your job is definitely easier if you have an upright or chest style freezer. Both of these types of freezers have their bonuses and downfalls. The upright freezer makes it easier to stack and find your meals, however, each time you open the door the cold "falls out" and your freezer will have to work harder, especially when you bombard it with many meals in one day. Having the cold "fall out" on a daily use basis as you get out a bag of peas or a box of ice cream is not harmful. The freezer motor is designed to keep the interior of the freezer at zero degrees. However, if you open the freezer door and let the cold "fall out" many times to add room temperature food, you risk having your freezer motor go on strike! A solution for this is to accumulate five or six meals and open your freezer fewer times. You could also collect the meals in the refrigerator to give them a chance to get cool before you put them in the freezer.

A chest style freezer contains the cold better as the cold will never fall out. However, the challenge is greater to stack things in a manner that makes the meals easy to retrieve without you falling in! There is a relatively simple solution to this, I have discovered, as I am in possession of a chest style freezer.

The first time I prepared many meals and desired to arrange them in my freezer, I was at first stumped until I noticed my kids' toy assortment in the garage. All the tennis balls, baseball gloves and swim fins were arranged in a three tier, stacking toy bin or utility bin. It consists of three baskets, stacked on top of each other with the front of each open to accommodate the toys. I dumped the toys on the garage floor (someone else can put them away - I'm cooking!) and lowered the whole thing into my freezer. It works beautifully!! The three baskets provide plenty of room for me to stack all the meals and all are easily accessible. These stacking, open shelf baskets can be found where organizer containers are sold. They can also be found at the large office supply stores.

The idea is to create vertical space in your chest style freezer. It is not important what you use, just that you create vertical space. A three tier stacking toy bin works great but so does a small plastic or metal bookshelf. Plastic crates, turned on their sides work well, too. Crates create cubicle vertical space. Chose crates that are not so big that the stacking area inside each crate is too high.

Plastic coated wire shelves are convenient to create vertical space. They snap together securely and come in many sizes. This allows you to create different configurations for your specific needs and freezer space.

For some, it is a common practice to fill cardboard boxes and stack them up in a chest freezer. This makes anything in the bottom box very difficult to retrieve. Don't sabotage your hard work by filling boxes and staking them one on top of the other, making the meals inconvenient and difficult to remove. You will use more space in your freezer if your food is accessible.

Whatever the style of your freezer, first spread the meals out in as much of a single layer as possible. Allow them to freeze or at least get very cold before stacking them on top of each other. Any liquid filled freezer bags, such as chicken soup, chili, taco soup or spaghetti sauce should be almost entirely frozen before stacking. Weight on the top of one of these liquid filled bags could cause too much pressure on the seam and cause it to break. Then you'll have a soupy mess in your freezer. You might also desire to not stack like meals together. Try putting an assortment of meals on each shelf.

One option to consider if you have an upright or chest freezer as well as a refrigerator freezer, is to store your meal-sized packages in the big freezer and store individual servings in the refrigerator freezer. Using different stacking shelves or containers to hold the individual servings makes this option especially efficient.

Remember the List of Recipes (Menu) you made when you chose your recipes? Use this list to keep track of what you have prepared and placed in your freezer. You can also mark the list with the location of each. Perhaps it is on the second shelf on the right. Or perhaps it is in the bottom blue crate.

As a meal is removed from the freezer, be sure to check it off the list. This way you will always know what you have in the freezer and be able to tell how soon you need to replenish your supply. Keeping a list of what is in your freezer and the location of each, will make finding and using what you have prepared a breeze, regardless of your freezer size or style.

Chapter 10

Thawing

Meals in freezer bags that have thawed can be conveniently poured into baking dishes for the oven, into dishes to be heated in the microwave, or into pans for heating on the stove top.

If you choose to thaw meals, they should be thawed in the refrigerator. Food that is allowed to come to room temperature can allow harmful bacteria to grow which can cause illness. It takes longer to thaw food in the refrigerator so some meals will need to be placed in the refrigerator to thaw the day before you plan to serve them. The larger, thicker and denser the frozen meal, the longer it will take to thaw. For example, frozen, uncooked chicken takes longer to thaw than cooked, shredded chicken in a recipe.

Most lunches from the freezer can be heated without thawing first. If the meal is packaged in a freezer bag, you may need to tear the bag in order to remove the food from the bag. Never microwave food in a plastic bag or bowl unless it is labeled **microwave safe.** I'm not a scientist but I have read articles that say that heating food in plastic, especially food that contains any fat, can overheat the plastic and cause toxins to be released into the food. You can't see, smell or taste the toxins but who knows? You could come down with some hideous ailment from toxins from overheated plastic! So, play it safe and remove the meal from the bag and place it in a microwave safe dish. Heat and stir until the food is hot and bubbly. Some soup recipes may require repeated heating and stirring until it is hot throughout. Some soups may require additional broth, cream or milk to thin to the consistency you desire.

Sandwich and salad fillings can usually be heated from frozen in a very short period of time. Usually just a minute or so in the microwave. The length of time is dependent upon the size of the serving and the power of the microwave.

Filled sandwiches and other baked items can be heated from frozen in the microwave but care must be taken to avoid overcooking. Crusts and bread doughs can become tough if heated too long in the microwave. If you desire a crisper crust place the thawed (even heated) portion in a toaster oven or under the broiler in the oven for a minute or two.

To be certain that a meal is completely hot, use an instant read thermometer. These look much like a meat thermometer but are not intended to be left in food when baking. Some have a dial and others are digital. Either one makes for a convenient and instant way to tell if a meal is ready to put on the table.

Chapter 11

Sample Order of Events

✔ **Gather Equipment**

✔ **Choose Recipes**

<u>**Slow Cooker**</u>
Zesty Beef and Vegetable Soup, page 95

<u>**Oven**</u>
BBQ Pork Sandwiches, page 124

<u>**StoveTop**</u>
Teriyaki Steak Bowls, page 147
Chile Cheese Soup, page 173

<u>**Oven Assemble**</u>
Pizza Roll-Ups, page 200
Chicken Squares, page 213

<u>**Assemble**</u>
Honey Mustard Turkey Burgers, page 231
BBQ Chicken Mini Pizzas, page 239
Italian Heroes, page 235
Beef Tacos, page 243

✔ **List Chosen Recipes**

✔ **Make Shopping List**

✔ **Shop**

✔ Arrange Recipe Cards

Arrange the recipe cards in the order you plan to prepare them. You may find it helpful to place the cards near the area you plan to prepare the food. Place the Slow Cooker recipe cards next to the slow cooker. If you are preparing more than one Slow Cooker recipe, you may want to start with the recipe with the shortest cooking time. If a recipe is still cooking in the slow cooker when you are finished with the other meals you are preparing for the day, it is easy to come back to the slow cooker later when it is done. If you start a recipe the night before cooking day, start the longest cooking recipe first so that it can cook all night and you won't have to turn it off in the middle of the night.

Place the Oven recipe cards beside the oven. If you are baking more than one Oven recipe start the recipe with the shortest baking time first, if possible. The order you bake the Oven recipes will depend on the baking time and temperature of the Oven Assemble recipes you choose. Try to coordinate baking both types of recipes to get the most efficient use of your oven. Only bake one Oven recipe at a time since you'll want to save room in the oven to be able to bake one Oven Assemble recipe at the same time.

Place both StoveTop recipe cards beside the stove. Start with the recipe that takes the longest. You could probably prepare both at the same time but it is easier to accomplish other tasks while only one StoveTop recipe is cooking. If you have two cooking on the stove top at the same time it can be difficult to do anything else except tend to them.

Place the Oven Assemble and Assemble recipe cards on the kitchen counter or next to the area you intend to assemble the recipes. Assemble the most difficult or time consuming recipes first, and save the easiest and quickest recipes for the end of your cooking day.

✔ **Make any "Day Before" preparations you have time for.**
- Arrange groceries for easy access.
- Get out any other needed items.
- Cook chicken for all recipes that call for cooked chicken.
- Chop onions for all recipes that call for chopped onion.
- Prepare any other needed vegetables.
- Shred cheese for all recipes that call for shredded cheese.

✔ **Cooking Day Order of Events**

1. If you did not cook the chicken the day before, put the chicken in large pot of salted water. Add 1 celery stalk, 1 carrot, 1 onion cut in half, and a few peppercorns. Boil slowly on a back burner until chicken is cooked through. When fully cooked, remove the chicken to cool but save the broth. Meanwhile....

2. Start **Zesty Beef & Vegetable Soup** on High in the slow cooker. Write down what time it will be in 6 hours.

3. Chop the onions, if you did not chop them the day before.

4. Shred all the cheese if it is not already shredded and/or if you did not shred it the day before.

5. Place **BBQ Pork Sandwiches** in the oven. Write down what time it will be in 3 hours.

6. If the chicken is cooked through, remove from heat, cool and chop or shred it into a bowl.

7. Start **Chile Cheese Soup** on the stove top. Set timer or write down what time it will be done.

8. Assemble **Chicken Squares**. Increase oven temperature to 350°. Put **Chicken Squares** in oven and set timer for 20 minutes.

9. When **Chile Cheese Soup** is done, remove from heat and set aside to cool.

10. When **Chicken Squares** are done remove from oven. Set aside to cool. Return oven temperature to 325°.

11. Start cooking steak for **Teriyaki Steak Bowls** on stove top.

12. Start rice for **Teriyaki Steak Bowls,** if you desire.

13. Prepare **Teriyaki Steak** sauce on stove top.

14. When steak is done, remove from stove top. Add sauce and set aside to cool.

15. Assemble **Pizza Roll-Ups.** Set aside to rise.

16. If **Chicken Squares** are cool, package them for the freezer, label and freeze.

17. When **Chile Cheese Soup** is cool, package it for the freezer, label and freeze.

18. Assemble **Italian Heroes.** Wrap, label and freeze.

19. If **BBQ Pork Sandwiches** are done, remove from oven. Set aside to cool. If they are not done, increase oven temperature to 350° and put **Pizza Roll-Ups** in the oven. Set timer for 20 minutes.

20. If **Teriyaki Steak Bowls** are cool, package them for the freezer, label and freeze.

21. Prepare **Beef Taco** filling. Allow to cool and place in freezer bag or package in individual servings for tacos, taco salad, burritos or tostadas. Label and freeze.

22. When done, remove **Pizza Roll-Ups** from oven.   Set aside to cool. If **BBQ Pork Sandwiches** are not done, return oven to 325°.

23. Assemble **BBQ Chicken Mini Pizzas**.   Place in the freezer in a single layer.

24. Assemble **Honey Mustard Turkey Burgers**.   Freeze.

25. Remove **BBQ Pork Sandwiches** from oven when it is done.   Slice pork and return to sauce. Set aside to cool.

26. When **Pizza Roll-Ups** are cool, package them for the freezer, label and freeze.

27. When **BBQ Pork Sandwiches** are cool, package them for the freezer, label and freeze.

28. When **Zesty Beef and Vegetable Soup** is done, remove it from the slow cooker and allow to cool.

29. When **Zesty Beef and Vegetable Soup** is cool, package it for the freezer, label and freeze.

30. When **BBQ Chicken Mini Pizzas** are frozen, transfer them to individual sandwich bags.   Place the wrapped pizzas in a gallon freezer bag.   Label and return to the freezer.

✔ **Admire your full freezer! Isn't it a beautiful thing?!**

Being prepared and organized, and utilizing multiple cooking methods at the same time is the most productive way to accomplish much in a short period of time.   However, preparing many lunches on the same day is not an exact science. This outline is only meant to be a guideline. It is intended to show you what is going on at the same time and what comes next. The time it takes to do particular tasks will vary from recipe to recipe, from cook to cook. Do not be discouraged if the process does not flow exactly as outlined. Some things may take longer and others may advance more quickly for you. This outline is intended to give you a general idea of the order of events.

Chapter 12

Other Options

To really make the most of your cooking experience, take advantage of sales as they come. When chicken goes on sale buy the amount of chicken you think you will need for cooking day, freeze it and have it on hand for when you are ready to cook. Likewise, buy up ground beef and other meats that you prefer to cook as they are on sale and store them in your freezer until you are ready to cook. Buying everything on the day before you cook leaves you at the mercy of the grocery store and you will pay whatever the price is that day, on sale or not.

Different sources will tell you that you cannot refreeze meat, because of the danger of the thawed meat coming to room temperature and allowing harmful bacteria to grow. Freezing does not kill the bacteria, it just postpones the day you get sick! You can refreeze meat as long as you never allow it to come to room temperature. Always thaw meat in the refrigerator and, preferably, use it while it still contains ice crystals.

While preparing 10 different recipes in one day provides a variety of lunches, it is certainly not your only option. You could choose to prepare a category of recipes. You could prepare many recipes of filled pastry sandwiches. Prepare different fillings and then prepare the doughs you desire to fill. Prepare them all in an assembly line fashion.

When spaghetti sauce goes on sale, make only recipes that use spaghetti sauce. Get your largest pan, perhaps it is your pressure canner, and prepare in it as much sauce as will fit. Assemble French Bread Pizza kits, individual pizzas, and filled pocket sandwiches.

You could choose to cook just chicken recipes when chicken is on sale. Then when ground beef goes on sale, prepare different burger and sandwich filling recipes.

There may be other times that you desire to prepare meals for your freezer but you do not have an entire day to devote to the process. There is no rule that says you *must* choose 10 recipes. Try choosing only 5. Do whatever you can do. Prepare only 2 or 3. Even if you only have time to prepare lunch today, be sure to at least double the recipe and freeze some.

There is no disguising the fact that preparing 10 recipes requires your undivided attention for a significant amount of the day. It is not overly difficult but it will require several hours to accomplish. However, it is important to remember that the time and effort you spend today will result in one day of freedom for each meal you place in the freezer. Also important to note is that preparing many meals in one day will consume much less time than preparing the same number of meals individually.

Chapter 13

Blessing the Lives of Others

Now that you know how to freeze food for your family, you are armed with knowledge that can help you bless the lives of others.

Meals frozen in disposable foil pans are very convenient for taking a meal into a neighbor or loved one. When you have meals in your freezer, no matter how busy you are, you can always choose a meal, effortlessly make it hot and ready to eat, and take it to a friend or loved one in need. The disposable pan makes for zero cleanup for them. They do not have the burden of returning a dish to you and you never lose another dish. This is a beautiful thing!

Don't overlook the value of single servings. As you package each recipe, consider packaging single servings. These are handy to take to work for lunch and/or on days you don't want macaroni and cheese for lunch, again.

Single servings could also bless the lives of others. Perhaps you have elderly parents, grandparents, elderly neighbors or other homebound loved ones. Whatever the situation, for those who have a difficult time preparing meals, consider how stocking their freezer could bless their lives. You could keep their freezer stocked with single servings, or meals for two.

One option is to devote an entire cooking day to preparing meals packaged for one or two. There will be no need to double recipes since, generally, a recipe for 6 will make three meals for two people, and even more single servings. Package the meals in small foil pans for one or two if it is a meal that is to be baked in the oven. Package all others in reusable plastic freezer containers. These can be easily microwaved, making for simple preparation for your loved one. If the meal is to be served with rice or pasta, place the rice or pasta in the container first and cover with the sauce or gravy, etc. This can also work with mashed potatoes if they are very thick.

Another option is to prepare meals for them at the same time that you freeze meals for your family. When you make your shopping list be sure to add an appropriate number of chicken pieces, etc. I have done this consistently for my husband's beloved grandmother. Every time I put meals in my freezer, I package two or three meals of each recipe for grandma. I place them all in a freezer basket in my chest freezer and then every other week or so I take some over and stack them in grandma's refrigerator freezer. This is helpful to her and keeps her from the painful task of standing for so long in the kitchen preparing meals for herself. It also spares her the expense and tedium of store bought frozen dinners.

A truly fun and beneficial option is to have a Baby Shower in which you make meals for the expectant mother. This is especially helpful to the mother who already has children. She probably already has baby booties and blankets. What she truly needs is meals in her freezer! This can be done different ways. One way is to freeze meals at home and each guest brings one or more meals for the expectant mother. Another option is to get together to make the meals. Everyone brings assigned items and you work together to cook and/or assemble the meals. The guest of honor goes home with the goods!

Chapter 14

Shortcuts

There are many time-saving shortcuts that can help you make the cooking and freezing process a smooth experience. As you prepare meals for the freezer, be alert to shortcuts that streamline the process and make it easier and time efficient. Make use of the following shortcuts that appeal to you, and add your own discoveries. Remember that there is not *one* specific way to prepare many meals in one day. These are guidelines. Make your own rules and change the process to fit your style and circumstances. Do not be a slave to directions.

✂ If you have cooked chicken for several recipes, divide the chicken into a bowl for each meal. Place the recipe card in front of the bowl and continue to add ingredients until that recipe is complete. Remember you will be cooking your chicken all at once for all the recipes that call for cooked chicken. Then you will be chopping or shredding the chicken. If you have three recipes that call for cooked, chopped chicken, divide your chicken among three bowls, rather than taking out chicken one recipe at a time and leaving to chance how much chicken you will actually have left for that last recipe. If you have many recipes that call for cooked chicken, divide the chicken in half. Leave one half in a large bowl, divide the other half among the three or four bowls.

✂ When making soup or other favorite recipes, consider making as much as your pan will hold and divide it into family-size and/or individual portions for the freezer. Do you find it frustrating to spend hours making your favorite soups, only to have them consumed in about six and a half minutes? Depending on your family size you may want to make more than double of a recipe. A huge pan of your favorite meal doesn't take much more time to prepare than a single meal of your favorite recipe. Make as much as your pan will hold and package it for the freezer in meal sized portions. You'll get six and a half minutes of pleasure many times over!

✂ Make enough of a soup or other recipes to freeze in both family-size portions and single serve portions. Family-size for occasions when every one is home, individual-size for lunch for one.

✂ When mincing fresh garlic use a metal garlic press. The plastic kind can break.

✂ Even easier and almost as good as fresh garlic is the bottled minced garlic that you can get in the produce section at the grocery store. It is in a small bottle next to the fresh garlic and it is usually very inexpensive. The same is true for ginger.

✂ When making stuffed pocket sandwiches, prepare some that are already baked and ready for the microwave, but also prepare some that are stuffed but unbaked. These are ready for the oven on a day you have a little more time and you desire the fabulous smells and goodness of freshly baked bread.

✂ When preparing burger recipes, freeze some that are ready to cook and freeze others that are already fully cooked. With the preparation already finished it is easy to put some burgers on the grill. If the burgers are already fully cooked it is easy to heat a burger for one or more in a moment's notice.

✄ If you want to prepare a recipe that calls for ham and you don't need to purchase a whole or half ham, just get what you need from the delicatessen at the grocery store. Ask the deli to cut an inch thick slice or two of ham. Deli ham is also great when a recipe calls for a few slices of ham.

✄ Mix and match pizza crust options and the topping recipes.

✄ Mix and match the doughs for stuffed pastries and the fillings.

✄ Consider using favorite sandwich filling recipes such as Sloppy Joes or BBQ Chicken to make great salads. Freeze the sandwich filling in single serving-sized portions in a muffin tin. Place salad greens in a bowl while the sandwich filling is heating. Toss together and drizzle with dressing. Delicious! and the varieties are endless.

✄ When preparing recipes that are usually served over rice, such as Teriyaki Chicken, freeze some in family-sized portions in freezer bags, ready to be heated while the rice is cooking. Freeze some in single serving-sized bowls, complete with rice on the bottom and chicken and sauce over the top. These are ready to heat and serve in a few minutes. They are wonderfully convenient to carry to work, too.

✄ If you prefer to use labels, make them the day before you need them. Print them out using the *30 Meals in One Day* computer program. Or tear or cut off strips of masking tape and stick them to the back of a cookie sheet(s). Write out your labels with name and cooking instructions. Place the labels on the table or wherever you choose to package your meals for the freezer. As each meal is packaged you can choose the appropriate label and attach it. Whether attaching to plastic or foil, be sure to attach each label *before* filling with food to be sure the labels adhere properly.

✄ Tape your List of Chosen Recipes (Menu) that you have prepared and placed in your freezer, on the door of the freezer, on the inside of a cupboard door or some other convenient place where you can refer to it often and keep it updated. This way, not only will you have a "menu," but you will also always know what you have in your freezer.

Use the shortcuts listed here that you find convenient. As you continue to freeze meals, you are sure to discover your own shortcuts that make your cooking experience more convenient and more enjoyable. Whatever method you settle on or whatever the number of recipes you decide to make, enjoy the journey! May your freezer always be full!

Chapter 15

Recipe Section

Slow Cooker Recipes

Slow Cooked Sloppy Joes

2 pounds lean ground beef
1 cup chopped onion
1 teaspoon salt
1/4 teaspoon pepper
1 (10.75-ounce) can chicken gumbo soup
2 tablespoons packed brown sugar
1/2 cup ketchup
1 tablespoon mustard

In a skillet, brown ground beef with onion, salt and pepper until beef is no longer pink. Place in slow cooker. Combine chicken gumbo soup, brown sugar, ketchup and mustard. Add to slow cooker and stir to combine. Cover and cook on Low for 8 hours or on High for 3 to 4 hours. Remove from slow cooker and allow to cool completely. Place in freezer bag or container. For individual servings, spray a muffin tin with non-stick cooking spray. Fill muffin cups with mixture. Cover and place pan in freezer just until frozen. Pop out and place in gallon freezer bag. Label and freeze. 12 servings.

To serve : Thaw and heat. Serve on hamburger buns.

Roast Beef Sandwiches

1 (4-pound) beef roast
1/2 cup packed brown sugar
1 (1.25-ounce) envelope onion soup mix
1 cup chopped onion
1/2 teaspoon garlic powder
1 teaspoon salt
1 teaspoon pepper

Trim roast of all visible fat. Cut roast into 6 pieces and place in slow cooker. Cover and cook on High for 3 hours. Drain broth, reserving 1 cup. Stir together reserved broth, brown sugar, onion soup mix, onion, garlic powder, salt and pepper. Pour over roast. Cover and cook on Low for 4 hours. Remove beef and allow to cool enough to handle. Shred and place in a large bowl. Pour sauce over shredded meat. Stir to coat. Allow to cool completely. Place in freezer bag or container. For individual servings, spray a muffin tin with non-stick cooking spray. Fill muffin cups with meat and sauce. Cover and place pan in freezer just until frozen. Pop out and place in gallon freezer bag. Label and freeze. 12 servings.

To serve: Thaw and heat. Serve on buns.

Ranch Hoagies

1 (3-pound) beef roast
1 cup chopped onion
1 (.7-ounce) envelope Ranch dressing mix

Trim roast of all visible fat. Cut roast in 4 pieces and place in slow cooker. Cover and cook on High for 2 hours. Drain broth, reserving 1 cup. Scatter onion over roast. Combine reserved broth with Ranch dressing mix. Pour over roast. Cover and cook on Low for 6 hours. Remove from slow cooker and allow to cool enough to handle. Shred meat and place in a large bowl. Pour sauce over shredded meat. Stir to coat. Allow to cool completely. Place in freezer bag or container. For individual servings, spray a muffin tin with non-stick cooking spray. Fill muffin cups with meat and sauce. Cover and place pan in freezer just until frozen. Pop out and place in gallon freezer bag. Label and freeze. 10 servings.

To serve: Thaw and heat. Serve on hoagie rolls. Top with lettuce and drizzle with **Ranch Dressing** (page 263).

 For a spicier version, substitute Zesty Italian dressing mix for the Ranch dressing mix.

Italian Beef

1 (3-pound) beef chuck roast
1 recipe **Italian Dressing** (page 264)

Trim roast of all visible fat. Cut roast into 4 pieces and place in slow cooker. Cover and cook on High for 3 hours. Drain broth. Prepare **Italian Dressing** and pour over beef. Cover and cook on Low for 3 hours. Remove roast from cooker. Shred or cut into thin slices. Return meat to sauce and stir to coat. Allow to cool completely. Place in freezer bag or container. For individual servings, spray a muffin tin with non-stick cooking spray. Fill muffin cups with meat and sauce. Cover and place pan in freezer just until frozen. Pop out and place in gallon freezer bag. Label and freeze. 10 servings.

To serve: Thaw and heat. Layer beef slices, Provolone cheese and bell pepper rings on Focaccia bread.

 Italian Beef makes great **Italian Beef Salad** (page 69).

Italian Beef Salad

1 recipe **Italian Beef** (page 68)
12 cups salad greens
1 (2.25-ounce) can sliced black olives, drained
1/2 cup sliced mushrooms
1/4 cup sliced green onions
1 tomato
1 cup shredded fresh Parmesan cheese
1 cup Italian croutons
Italian Dressing (page 264)

Prepare **Italian Beef** as directed. Allow to cool completely. Place in freezer bag or container. To freeze filling for individual salad servings, spray cups of a muffin tin with nonstick cooking spray. Fill cups with filling. Press down gently. Cover and freeze. When frozen, pop out and place in a gallon freezer bag. Label and freeze. 6 servings.

To serve: In large salad bowl (or in individual bowls), toss together salad greens, black olives, mushrooms and green onions. Cut tomato into wedges and add to salad. Heat **Italian Beef** and pile on top. Sprinkle Parmesan cheese and Italian croutons over all. Serve with **Italian Dressing**.

To make Italian croutons, trim crusts from 2 slices of white bread. Generously butter both sides of the bread slices. Sprinkle with Italian seasoning. Cut into 1/2-inch cubes. Arrange cubes on an ungreased baking sheet. Bake at 400° for 10 to 15 minutes, stirring occasionally, until golden brown and crisp.

Ranch French Dip

1 (4-pound) beef roast
1/2 cup soy sauce
1 teaspoon beef bouillon
1 (10.5-ounce) can beef consommé
1 (.7-ounce) envelope Ranch dressing mix
3 whole peppercorns
1 teaspoon garlic powder

Trim roast of all visible fat. Cut roast in 4 pieces and place in slow cooker. Combine soy sauce, bouillon, beef consommé, Ranch dressing mix, peppercorns and garlic powder. Pour over roast. Cover and cook on Low for 10 hours. Remove meat and allow to cool enough to handle. Remove and discard peppercorns. Shred or slice beef and place in a large bowl. Pour sauce over shredded meat. Stir to coat. Allow to cool completely. Place in freezer bag or container. For individual servings, spray a muffin tin with non-stick cooking spray. Fill muffin cups with meat and sauce. Cover and place pan in freezer just until frozen. Pop out and place in gallon freezer bag. Label and freeze. 12 servings.

To serve: Thaw and heat. Drain broth and serve in bowls for dipping. Serve meat on French rolls.

Corned Beef Melts

1 (4-pound) corned beef brisket
1 cup apple cider
1/4 cup packed brown sugar
2 teaspoons grated orange peel
2 teaspoons mustard
dash allspice
3 whole cloves
1 onion
2 carrots

Trim excess fat from corned beef. Place meat in a slow cooker. Combine apple cider, brown sugar, orange peel, mustard, allspice and cloves. Pour over meat. Cut onion into 4 pieces and add to slow cooker. Cut carrots into 6 pieces and add to slow cooker. Cover and cook on Low for 10 hours. Remove meat from cooker and allow to cool enough to handle. Discard onion and carrots. Pull meat into chunks. Place in freezer bag with enough liquid to moisten meat. For individual servings, spray a muffin tin with non-stick cooking spray. Pack muffin cups with meat. Spoon one tablespoon of broth into each. Cover and place pan in freezer just until frozen. Pop out and place in gallon freezer bag. Label and freeze. 12 servings.

To serve: Thaw and heat. Pile meat onto buns. Top with Swiss cheese. Broil until cheese melts. Top with sauerkraut. Drizzle with **Simple Thousand Island Dressing** (page 269).

Swiss Steak Sandwiches

2 pounds beef round steak
1 tablespoon canola oil
1/2 cup chopped celery
1 cup chopped onion
3/4 cup beef broth
1/2 cup tomato sauce
1/4 cup water
1/4 cup sugar
2 tablespoons onion soup mix
1 tablespoon apple cider vinegar

Cut round steak into about 6 pieces. In a large skillet, brown steak in oil. Transfer to slow cooker. In the same skillet, cook celery and onion for about 1 minute. Gradually add broth, tomato sauce, and water, stirring to loosen brown bits on bottom of pan. Add sugar, onion soup mix and vinegar. Cook and stir until mixture begins to boil. Pour over steak in slow cooker. Cover and cook on Low for 8 hours. Remove from slow cooker and allow to cool enough to handle. Shred meat and place in a large bowl. Pour sauce over shredded meat. Stir to coat. Allow to cool completely. Place in freezer bag or container. For individual servings, spray a muffin tin with non-stick cooking spray. Fill muffin cups with meat and sauce. Cover and place pan in freezer just until frozen. Pop out and place in gallon freezer bag. Label and freeze. 8 servings.

To serve: Thaw and heat. Serve on toasted buns.

Smoky Barbeque

1 (3-pound) beef chuck roast
2 1/2 cups ketchup
2 cups red wine vinegar
1 cup packed brown sugar
1/2 cup molasses
1 tablespoon liquid smoke
1 teaspoon garlic salt
1/2 teaspoon onion powder
1/4 teaspoon pepper

Trim roast of all visible fat. Cut roast into 4 pieces and place in slow cooker. Cover and cook on High for 2 hours. Drain broth. Meanwhile, in a large saucepan, combine ketchup, vinegar, brown sugar, molasses, liquid smoke, garlic salt, onion powder and pepper. Whisk until smooth. Bring to a boil. Reduce heat and simmer for about 30 minutes or until thick and reduced to about 3 cups. Pour 1 cup barbeque sauce over beef. Cover and cook on Low for 6 hours. Remove roast from slow cooker. Allow to cool enough to handle. Shred beef. Place shredded beef in a large bowl. Add 1 cup of sauce from slow cooker and remaining 2 cups barbeque sauce. Stir to coat. Allow to cool completely. Place in freezer bag or container. For individual servings, spray a muffin tin with non-stick cooking spray. Fill muffin cups with meat and sauce. Cover and place pan in freezer just until frozen. Pop out and place in gallon freezer bag. Label and freeze. 10 servings.

To serve: Thaw and heat. Serve on toasted rolls. Top with shredded lettuce and shredded cheese.

 Substitute 3 pounds boneless skinless chicken thighs for chuck roast to make delicious **Smoky Chicken Barbeque**.

Honey Barbeque

1 (3-pound) beef chuck roast
1 (24-ounce) bottle barbeque sauce
1/2 cup honey
1/3 cup Worcestershire sauce
1 teaspoon mustard
1/2 cup chopped onion
1 teaspoon salt
1/4 teaspoon pepper

Trim roast of all visible fat. Cut roast in 4 pieces and place in slow cooker. Cover and cook on High for 2 hours. Drain broth. Combine barbeque sauce, honey, Worcestershire sauce, mustard, onion, salt and pepper. Pour over roast in slow cooker. Cover and cook on Low for 6 hours. Remove roast and allow to cool enough to handle. Shred or chop meat and place in a large bowl. Pour sauce over shredded meat. Stir to coat. Allow to cool completely. Place in freezer bag or container. For individual servings, spray a muffin tin with non-stick cooking spray. Fill muffin cups with meat and sauce. Cover and place pan in freezer just until frozen. Pop out and place in gallon freezer bag. Label and freeze. 10 servings.

To serve: Thaw and heat. Serve on toasted buns with shredded lettuce and dill pickles.

Substitute 3 pounds of boneless skinless chicken thighs for the chuck roast for delicious **Honey Barbeque Chicken.**

Root Beer Barbeque

1 (3-pound) pork sirloin roast
1 cup root beer
1/2 teaspoon salt
1/2 teaspoon pepper
2 cups onion wedges
2 tablespoons minced garlic
2 (12-ounce) cans root beer
1 (12-ounce) bottle chili sauce

Trim any visible fat from roast. Cut roast into 4 pieces and place in slow cooker. Pour 1 cup root beer over roast. Sprinkle meat with the salt and pepper. Add onions and garlic. Cover and cook on Low for 8 to 10 hours or on High for 4 to 5 hours. In a medium saucepan combine root beer and chili sauce. Bring to a boil. Reduce heat. Boil gently, uncovered, stirring occasionally, about 30 minutes or until mixture is reduced to 2 cups. Remove roast and onions from slow cooker. Allow to cool enough to handle. Discard broth. Shred meat and combine with onions. Pour root beer sauce over all. Stir to coat. Allow to cool completely. Place in freezer bag or container. For individual servings, spray a muffin tin with non-stick cooking spray. Fill muffin cups with meat and sauce. Cover and place pan in freezer just until frozen. Pop out and place in gallon freezer bag. Label and freeze. 10 servings.

To serve: Thaw and heat. Line buns with lettuce leaves and tomato slices. Add meat, onions and sauce.

Apricot Pork Sandwiches

1 (3-pound) pork roast
1/3 cup chopped dried apricots
1 cup chopped onion
2 teaspoons minced garlic
1 (18-ounce) jar apricot preserves
1 (10.75-ounce) can French onion soup
2 tablespoons mustard
1/2 teaspoon salt
1/8 teaspoon pepper

Trim any visible fat from roast. Cut roast into 4 pieces and place in slow cooker. Cover and cook on High for 2 hours. Drain liquid. Add dried apricots, onion and garlic to slow cooker. Combine apricot preserves, French onion soup, mustard, salt and pepper. Add to slow cooker. Cover and cook on Low for 8 hours. Remove roast and allow to cool enough to handle. Shred or chop meat and place in a large bowl. Pour sauce over shredded meat. Stir to coat. Allow to cool completely. Place in freezer bag or container. For individual servings, spray a muffin tin with non-stick cooking spray. Fill muffin cups with meat and sauce. Cover and place pan in freezer just until frozen. Pop out and place in gallon freezer bag. Label and freeze. 10 servings.

To serve: Thaw and heat. Serve on toasted buns with shredded lettuce.

To toast buns, split buns and spread with butter. Set oven to broil. Place buns, buttered side up, on baking sheet. Broil 4 inches from heat for 1 to 2 minutes, until golden brown. Watch carefully, they brown rapidly.

Catalina Buns

2 pounds boneless pork ribs
1 cup chopped onion
2 teaspoons minced garlic
1 cup **Catalina Dressing** (page 265)

Place ribs in slow cooker. Cover and cook on High for 3 hours. Drain broth. Add onion and garlic. Prepare dressing and pour dressing over all. Cover and reduce heat to Low. Cook for 3 hours. Remove ribs from slow cooker and allow to cool enough to handle. Shred ribs and place in a large bowl. Pour sauce over shredded meat. Stir to coat. Allow to cool completely. Place in freezer bag or container. For individual servings, spray a muffin tin with non-stick cooking spray. Fill muffin cups with meat and sauce. Cover and place pan in freezer just until frozen. Pop out and place in gallon freezer bag. Label and freeze. 8 servings.

To serve: Thaw and heat. Serve on buns.

For delicious **Catalina Salad**, serve warm shredded meat on salad greens. Top with red onion and **Catalina Dressing**.

Tangy Beef BBQ

1 (4-pound) beef chuck roast
3 cups chopped celery
1 cup chopped onion
1 cup ketchup
1 cup barbeque sauce
2 tablespoons apple cider vinegar
2 tablespoons Worcestershire sauce
2 tablespoons packed brown sugar
1 teaspoon chili powder
1 teaspoon salt
1/2 teaspoon pepper
1/2 teaspoon garlic powder

Trim roast of all visible fat. Cut roast in 6 pieces and place in slow cooker. Cover and cook on High for 2 hours. Drain broth. Combine celery, onion, ketchup, barbeque sauce, vinegar, Worcestershire sauce, brown sugar, chili powder, salt, pepper and garlic powder. Pour over roast. Cover and cook on High for 6 hours. Remove roast and allow to cool enough to handle. Shred meat and place in a large bowl. Pour sauce over shredded meat. Stir to coat. Allow to cool completely. Place in freezer bag or container. For individual servings, spray a muffin tin with non-stick cooking spray. Fill muffin cups with meat and sauce. Cover and place pan in freezer just until frozen. Pop out and place in gallon freezer bag. Label and freeze. 12 servings.

To serve: Thaw and heat. Serve on buns. Top with shredded lettuce.

Beef Barbeque

1 (3-pound) beef roast
1 cup chopped onion
1 (12-ounce) bottle chili sauce
1 cup ketchup
1 tablespoon Worcestershire sauce
3 tablespoons apple cider vinegar
1/8 teaspoon pepper
1/2 teaspoon salt
1/3 cup packed brown sugar
2 teaspoons ground mustard

Cut beef roast into 1-inch cubes. Place beef cubes in slow cooker. Cover and cook on High for 2 hours. Drain broth. Combine onion, chili sauce, ketchup, Worcestershire sauce, vinegar, pepper, salt, brown sugar and ground mustard. Add to slow cooker and stir. Cover and cook on High for 4 hours. Stir to partially shred beef. Remove from slow cooker and allow to cool completely. Place in freezer bag or container. For individual servings, spray a muffin tin with non-stick cooking spray. Fill muffin cups with meat and sauce. Cover and place pan in freezer just until frozen. Pop out and place in gallon freezer bag. Label and freeze. 10 servings.

To serve: Thaw and heat. Serve on bulky rolls.

Combo Barbeque

1 1/2 pounds cubed beef stew meat
1 1/2 pounds cubed lean pork
1 cup finely chopped onion
2 cups finely chopped green bell pepper
1(6-ounce) can tomato paste
1/2 cup packed brown sugar
1/4 cup apple cider vinegar
1 tablespoon chili powder
1 teaspoon salt
2 teaspoons Worcestershire sauce
1 teaspoon ground mustard

Place beef and pork in slow cooker. Cover and cook on High for 2 hours. Drain broth. Scatter onion and green bell pepper over meat. Combine tomato paste, brown sugar, vinegar, chili powder, salt, Worcestershire sauce and ground mustard. Add to slow cooker and stir into meat and vegetables. Cover and cook on High for 6 hours. Stir to partially shred meat. Remove from slow cooker and allow to cool completely . Place in freezer bag or container. For individual servings, spray a muffin tin with non-stick cooking spray. Fill muffin cups with meat and sauce. Cover and place pan in freezer just until frozen. Pop out and place in gallon freezer bag. Label and freeze. 10 servings.

To serve: Thaw and heat. Serve on buttered rolls or in pita bread. Top with shredded lettuce and shredded cheese.

 For a main dish variation, **Combo Barbeque** is delicious served over rice.

Chicken Barbeque

3 pounds boneless skinless chicken thighs
1 cup ketchup
3/4 cup packed brown sugar
3 tablespoons Worcestershire sauce
1 teaspoon garlic salt
1/4 teaspoon pepper

Place chicken in slow cooker. Cover and cook on High for 2 hours. Drain broth. Combine ketchup, brown sugar, Worcestershire sauce, garlic salt and pepper. Pour over chicken. Cook on High for 2 hours or on Low for 4 hours. Remove chicken and allow to cool enough to handle. Shred chicken and place in a large bowl. Pour sauce over shredded meat. Stir to coat. Allow to cool completely. Place in freezer bag or container. For individual servings, spray a muffin tin with non-stick cooking spray. Fill muffin cups with meat and sauce. Cover and place pan in freezer just until frozen. Pop out and place in gallon freezer bag. Label and freeze. 10 servings.

To serve: Thaw and heat. Serve on buns.

 For a main dish variation, serve **Chicken Barbeque** over rice.

BBQ Turkey Sandwiches

3 cups cooked, chopped turkey
1/2 cup chopped onion
1 teaspoon minced garlic
1 cup ketchup
1/3 cup packed brown sugar
1/4 teaspoon chili powder
1/2 teaspoon salt
1/8 teaspoon pepper
1 tablespoon apple cider vinegar

Place turkey, onion and garlic in slow cooker. Combine ketchup, brown sugar, chili powder, salt, pepper and vinegar. Pour over turkey. Stir to combine. Cook on High for 3 hours or on Low for 6 to 8 hours. Remove from slow cooker and allow to cool completely. Place in freezer bag or container. For individual servings, spray a muffin tin with non-stick cooking spray. Fill muffin cups with meat and sauce. Cover and place pan in freezer just until frozen. Pop out and place in gallon freezer bag. Label and freeze. 6 servings.

To serve: Thaw and heat. Serve on buns or in pita pockets. Top with shredded lettuce and sliced avocado.

Teriyaki Turkey Sandwiches

1 1/2 pounds boneless skinless turkey breast
3/4 cup teriyaki sauce
1/4 cup orange marmalade
1/4 teaspoon pepper

Place turkey in slow cooker. Combine teriyaki sauce, marmalade and pepper. Pour over turkey. Cover and cook on Low for 8 hours. Remove turkey and shred. Return to sauce and mix well. Allow to cool completely. Place in freezer bag or container. For individual servings, spray a muffin tin with non-stick cooking spray. Fill muffin cups with meat and sauce. Cover and place pan in freezer just until frozen. Pop out and place in gallon freezer bag. Label and freeze. 6 servings.

To serve: Thaw and heat. Spoon onto warm rolls. Top with lettuce.

Saucy Ham Buns

2 (10.75-ounce) cans tomato soup
3 tablespoons white vinegar
1/4 cup packed brown sugar
2 tablespoons Worcestershire sauce
2 pounds deli sliced honey baked ham

In slow cooker, combine soup, vinegar, brown sugar and Worcestershire sauce. Mix well. Cut ham into 1/2-inch wide strips. Add to slow cooker. Mix to coat. Cover and cook on Low for 3 hours. Allow to cool. Place in freezer bag or container. For individual servings, spray a muffin tin with non-stick cooking spray. Fill muffin cups with meat and sauce. Cover and place pan in freezer just until frozen. Pop out and place in gallon freezer bag. Label and freeze. 8 servings.

To serve: Thaw and heat. Serve on toasted buns. Top with American cheese and shredded lettuce.

For perfect toasted buns, split buns and spread butter on cut side. Heat griddle to 375°. Place buns, buttered side down, on hot griddle, just until golden brown.

Slow Cooked Chicken Fajitas

3 pounds boneless skinless chicken breast
1 cup sliced green bell pepper
1 cup sliced red bell pepper
1 cup sliced onion
2 tablespoons packed brown sugar
3 teaspoons minced garlic
2 teaspoons cumin
2 teaspoons coriander
1 teaspoon salt
1/2 teaspoon pepper
2 tablespoons lime juice
2 tablespoons Worcestershire sauce

Place chicken in slow cooker. Cover and cook on High for 2 hours. Drain broth. Top with sliced red pepper, green pepper and onion. Add garlic, cumin, coriander, salt, pepper, lime juice and Worcestershire sauce. Cover and cook on Low for 8 hours. Remove chicken and allow to cool enough to handle. Shred chicken and place in a large bowl. Pour sauce and vegetables over shredded meat. Stir to coat. Allow to cool completely. Place in freezer bag or container. For individual servings, spray a muffin tin with non-stick cooking spray. Fill muffin cups with meat and sauce. Cover and place pan in freezer just until frozen. Pop out and place in gallon freezer bag. Label and freeze. 10 servings.

To serve: Thaw and heat. Spoon onto center of warm tortillas. Top with sour cream and salsa. Roll up and serve.

Slow Cooked Beef Fajitas

1 1/2 pounds beef round steak
2 tablespoons canola oil
2 tablespoons lemon juice
1 teaspoon minced garlic
1 1/2 teaspoons cumin
1 teaspoon seasoned salt
1/2 teaspoon chili powder
1/4 teaspoon crushed red pepper flakes
1 cup sliced green bell pepper
1 cup sliced onion

Cut steak into thin strips. In a skillet over medium heat, brown the steak in oil. Place steak and drippings in a slow cooker. Add lemon juice, garlic, cumin, salt, chili powder and red pepper flakes. Mix well. Cover and cook on High for 3 hours. Add green pepper and onion. Cover and cook for 1 hour or until vegetables are tender. Remove from slow cooker and allow to cool completely. Place in freezer bag or container. For individual servings, spray a muffin tin with non-stick cooking spray. Fill muffin cups with mixture. Cover and place pan in freezer just until frozen. Pop out and place in gallon freezer bag. Label and freeze. 6 servings.

To serve: Thaw and heat. Spoon beef and vegetables down the center of warm tortillas. Top each with cheese, salsa, sour cream, lettuce and tomatoes. Roll up and serve.

Beef Fajitas Salad

1 recipe **Slow Cooked Beef Fajitas** (page 86)
12 cups torn Iceburg lettuce
1/2 cup sliced red bell pepper
1/2 cup sliced green bell pepper
1/2 cup sliced onion
1 avocado
Avocado Dressing (page 272)

Prepare **Slow Cooked Beef Fajitas** as directed. Allow to cool completely. Place in freezer bag or container. To freeze filling for individual salad servings, spray cups of a muffin tin with non-stick cooking spray. Fill cups with filling. Press down gently. Cover and freeze. When frozen, pop out and place in a gallon freezer bag. Label and freeze. 6 servings.

To serve: In large salad bowl (or in individual bowls), toss together lettuce, red bell pepper, green bell pepper and onion. Peel and slice avocado and arrange over salad. Heat **Beef Fajitas** and add to salad. Serve with **Avocado Dressing**.

To peel an avocado, using a sharp knife, cut avocado in half lengthwise, down to the seed. Gently twist and pull halves apart. Tap the seed with the edge of a knife and lift the seed out. Slide a spoon just under the thick skin to remove the avocado.

For Chicken Fajitas Salad, substitute **Slow Cooked Chicken Fajitas** (page 85).

Beef and Chicken Fajitas

1 1/2 pounds beef flank steak
1 1/2 pounds boneless skinless chicken breast
1 cup chopped onion
1 cup chopped green bell pepper
1 (4-ounce) can diced jalapeño pepper
1 tablespoon chopped cilantro
2 teaspoons minced garlic
1 teaspoon chili powder
1 teaspoon cumin
1 teaspoon coriander
1/2 teaspoon salt
1 (15-ounce) can Mexican tomatoes

Cut flank steak into 6 pieces. Place beef and chicken in slow cooker. Cover and cook on High for 2 hours. Drain broth. Combine onion, green pepper, jalapeño pepper, cilantro, garlic, chili powder, cumin, coriander, salt and tomatoes. Pour over meat. Cover and cook on Low for 8 hours or on High for 4 to 5 hours. Remove meat from slow cooker and allow to cool enough to handle. Shred meat and place in a large bowl. Pour sauce and vegetables over shredded meat. Stir to coat. Allow to cool completely. Place in freezer bag or container. For individual servings, spray a muffin tin with non-stick cooking spray. Fill muffin cups with meat and sauce. Cover and place pan in freezer just until frozen. Pop out and place in gallon freezer bag. Label and freeze. 6 servings.

To serve: Thaw and heat. Spoon down center of warm tortillas. Top with sour cream, guacamole, shredded cheese and salsa. Roll up and serve.

 For milder fajitas, substitute 1 (4-ounce) can diced green chiles for the jalapeño peppers.

Cheesy Chicken Burritos

3 pounds boneless skinless chicken breast
1 (12-ounce) jar salsa
1 (10.75-ounce) can of cream of chicken soup
1 (4-ounce) can of diced green chiles
1 cup shredded Cheddar cheese
1/2 cup shredded Monterey Jack cheese
1/2 cup chopped onion
1 (2.25-ounce) can sliced black olives

Place chicken in slow cooker. Cover and cook on High for 2 hours. Drain broth. Combine salsa, cream of chicken soup, green chiles, onion and drained black olives. Pour over chicken. Stir in cheese. Cover and cook on Low for 3 hours. Remove chicken and allow to cool enough to handle. Shred chicken and place in a large bowl. Pour sauce over shredded meat. Stir to coat. Allow to cool completely. Place in freezer bag or container. For individual servings, spray a muffin tin with non-stick cooking spray. Fill muffin cups with meat and sauce. Cover and place pan in freezer just until frozen. Pop out and place in gallon freezer bag. Label and freeze. 10 servings.

To serve: Thaw and heat. Spoon onto warm tortillas. Roll up and serve or top with shredded lettuce, sour cream and salsa.

Chicken Tacos

4 pounds boneless skinless chicken breast
1 (1.25-ounce) envelope taco seasoning
1 (4-ounce) can diced green chiles

Place chicken in slow cooker. Cover and cook on High for 2 hours. Drain broth. Scatter undrained green chiles over chicken. Sprinkle taco seasoning over all. Cover and cook on Low for 6 hours. Remove chicken and allow to cool enough to handle. Shred chicken. Return to slow cooker and mix well. Remove from slow cooker and allow to cool completely. Place in freezer bag or container. For individual servings, spray a muffin tin with non-stick cooking spray. Fill muffin cups with meat. Cover and place pan in freezer just until frozen. Pop out and place in gallon freezer bag. Label and freeze. 12 servings.

To serve: Thaw and heat. Serve on warmed tortillas with salsa, sour cream, black olives, lettuce and toma-toes.

 Chicken Tacos also makes fabulous **Taco Salad** (page 248). `

Bean and Chicken Tacos

1 1/2 pounds boneless skinless chicken thighs
1 (8-ounce) can tomato sauce
1 (4-ounce) can diced green chiles
1 cup chopped onion
1 teaspoon chili powder
1 (1.25-ounce) envelope taco seasoning
1 (15-ounce) can cannellini beans

Place chicken in slow cooker. Top with tomato sauce, green chiles and onion. Sprinkle with chili powder and taco seasoning. Pour drained beans over all and stir. Cover and cook on low for 8 hours. Remove chicken and shred. Mash some of the beans with a potato masher. Return shredded chicken to slow cooker and mix well. Remove from slow cooker and allow to cool completely. Place in freezer bag or container. For individual servings, spray a muffin tin with non-stick cooking spray. Fill muffin cups. Cover and place pan in freezer just until frozen. Pop out and place in gallon freezer bag. Label and freeze. 10 servings.

To serve: Thaw and heat. Spoon into heated taco shells. Top with cheese, lettuce, salsa and sour cream.

 Bean and Chicken Tacos also makes great burritos. Serve hot filling in warm flour tortillas.

BBQ Pork Tacos

1 (3-pound) pork roast
1 cup sliced onion
2 cups barbeque sauce
3/4 cup salsa
3 tablespoons chili powder
1 tablespoon **Taco Seasoning** (page 288)

Trim roast of all visible fat. Cut roast into 4 pieces and place in slow cooker. Top with onion. Cover and cook on High for 2 hours. Drain broth. Combine barbeque sauce, salsa, chili powder and taco seasoning. Pour over pork. Cover and cook on Low for 8 hours. Remove from cooker. Allow to cool enough to handle. Shred pork and place in a large bowl. Pour sauce over shredded meat. Stir to coat. Allow to cool completely. Place in freezer bag or container. For individual servings, spray a muffin tin with non-stick cooking spray. Fill muffin cups with meat and sauce. Cover and place pan in freezer just until frozen. Pop out and place in gallon freezer bag. Label and freeze. 10 servings.

To serve: Thaw and heat. Spoon into heated taco shells. Top with cheese, lettuce, salsa and sour cream.

 BBQ Pork Tacos also makes great **Taco Salad** (page 248).

Green Chile Burritos

1 (3-pound) pork roast
1 cup chopped onion
1 (1-ounce) envelope pork gravy mix
1 (1-ounce) envelope onion gravy mix
3 (4-ounce) cans diced green chiles

Trim roast of all visible fat. Cut roast into 4 pieces and place in slow cooker. Cover and cook on High for 2 hours. Drain, reserving 1 1/2 cups broth. Scatter onions and green chiles over roast. In a saucepan, combine reserved broth, pork gravy mix and onion gravy mix. Heat to boiling. Pour over roast. Cover and cook on Low for 6 hours. Remove roast and allow to cool enough to handle. Shred meat and place in a large bowl. Pour sauce over shredded meat. Stir to coat. Allow to cool completely. Place in freezer bag or container. For individual servings, spray a muffin tin with non-stick cooking spray. Fill muffin cups with meat and sauce. Cover and place pan in freezer just until frozen. Pop out and place in gallon freezer bag. Label and freeze. 10 servings.

To serve: Thaw and heat. Serve wrapped in warm flour or corn tortillas. Top with sour cream.

BBQ Bean Soup

1 pound dry Great Northern beans
2 pounds beef short ribs
1 cup chopped onion
1/8 teaspoon pepper
6 cups beef broth
2 teaspoons salt
1 cup **BBQ Sauce** (page 280)

Cover beans with water and soak overnight. Drain and discard water. In a saucepan, cover beans with water and boil 10 minutes. Drain and discard water. Place beans and beef cubes in slow cooker. Add onion, pepper and beef broth. Cover and cook on Low for 10 to 12 hours. Remove short ribs and cut meat from bones. Return meat to slow cooker. Stir in BBQ Sauce and salt. Remove from slow cooker and allow to cool completely. Place in freezer bag or in containers for individual servings. Label and freeze. 8 servings.

To serve: Thaw, heat and serve.

Zesty Beef and Vegetable Soup

1 pound cubed beef stew meat
1/2 cup chopped onion
2 teaspoons minced garlic
2 cups shredded cabbage
2 cups frozen corn
2 cups frozen green beans
2 cups sliced carrots
4 cups hot and spicy tomato vegetable juice
1 (15-ounce) can Italian tomatoes
2 tablespoons Worcestershire sauce
1 teaspoon basil
1 tablespoon sugar
1 teaspoon salt
1/4 teaspoon pepper

Place beef in slow cooker. Add onion, garlic, shredded cabbage, corn, green beans and carrots. Combine tomato vegetable juice, stewed tomatoes, Worcestershire sauce, basil, sugar, salt and pepper. Pour into slow cooker and stir to combine. Cover and cook on Low for 8 to 10 hours or on High for 6 hours. Remove from slow cooker and allow to cool completely. Place in freezer bag or in containers for individual servings. Label and freeze. 8 servings.

To serve: Thaw, heat and serve.

Cheese and Meatball Soup

2 cups beef broth
1 cup frozen corn
1 cup cubed potato
1 cup sliced celery
1/2 cup sliced carrot
1/2 cup chopped onion
1 teaspoon salt
1/4 teaspoon pepper
1 (16-ounce) jar processed American cheese
1 pound lean ground beef
1/4 cup dry bread crumbs
1 egg, lightly beaten
1/2 teaspoon salt
1/2 teaspoon hot pepper sauce

In slow cooker, combine beef broth, corn, potato, celery, carrot, onion, salt and pepper. In a bowl, combine ground beef, bread crumbs, egg, salt and hot pepper sauce. Mix ingredients together thoroughly. Shape into 3/4-inch meatballs. Place uncooked meatballs in slow cooker. Stir gently. Cover and cook on Low for 8 to 10 hours. Add cheese and stir gently until melted and well blended. Remove from slow cooker and allow to cool completely. Place in freezer bag or in containers for individual servings. Label and freeze. 8 servings.

To serve: Thaw. Heat and stir until smooth. Add a little broth to thin soup, if desired.

Chicken Vegetable Soup

1 pound boneless skinless chicken breast
1 (10-ounce) package frozen green beans
1 (10-ounce) package frozen corn
1 cup chopped onion
1 cup sliced carrots
1 cup sliced zucchini
2 teaspoons minced garlic
6 cups chicken broth
1 (6-ounce) can tomato paste
2 bay leaves
1 tablespoon sugar
1 teaspoon salt
3 whole peppercorns

Cut chicken into 1-inch cubes. Place in slow cooker. Add green beans, corn, onion, carrots, zucchini and garlic. Combine chicken broth, tomato paste, bay leaves, sugar, salt and peppercorns. Pour over chicken and vegetables. Stir to combine. Cover and cook on Low for 8 to 10 hours or on High for 5 hours. Remove from slow cooker and allow to cool completely. Remove bay leaves and peppercorns. Place in freezer bag or in containers for individual servings. Label and freeze. 8 servings.

To serve: Thaw, heat and serve.

Monterey Clam Chowder

1/2 pound chopped bacon
1/2 cup butter
1 cup sliced carrot
1 cup chopped onion
1 cup diced potato
1/2 cup sliced celery
1 1/2 cups flour
4 cups chicken broth
2 cups milk
2 cups cream
2 cups half-and-half
3 teaspoons minced garlic
1/2 teaspoon pepper
3 (6.5-ounce) cans chopped clams

In a skillet over medium heat, cook bacon until starting to brown. Add butter to skillet. Add carrots, onion, potato and celery. Cook and stir until vegetables are tender but not brown. When vegetables are tender, add flour. Cook for about two minutes, allowing flour to cook while stirring occasionally. Add chicken broth, milk, cream and half-and-half. Cook and stir until smooth and bubbly. Add garlic, pepper and chopped clams. Transfer to slow cooker. Cover and cook on Low for 3 hours. Remove from slow cooker and allow to cool completely. Place in freezer bag or in containers for individual servings. Label and freeze. 8 servings.

To serve: Thaw. Heat and stir until smooth. Thin soup with a little chicken broth, milk or cream, if desired.

Caramelized French Onion Soup

3 pounds sweet onions (Walla Walla or Vidalia)
1 (10.5-ounce) can beef broth
1/4 cup butter
1 (10.5-ounce) can beef consommé
1 (10.5-ounce) can beef broth
2 cup water
1 tablespoon sugar
1/2 teaspoon salt

Cut onions in half. Cut halves into 1/2-inch thick slices. Place in slow cooker. Add beef broth and butter. Cover and cook on High for 8 hours or until golden brown and very soft. Combine beef consommé, beef broth, water, sugar and salt. Pour over onions. Cover and cook on High for 2 1/2 hours. Remove from slow cooker and allow to cool completely. Place in freezer bag or in containers for individual servings. Label and freeze. 6 servings.

To serve: Thaw and heat. Ladle soup into oven proof bowl(s). Top with toasted French bread and shredded Swiss cheese. Place bowl(s) on baking sheet. Broil until cheese is melted and just starting to brown. Serve immediately.

Instead of French bread, try topping soup with an extra-large crouton. To make extra-large crouton, butter half of a hamburger bun. Broil in oven or in toaster oven until golden brown.

Oven Recipes

French Dip

1 (4-pound) beef roast
1/2 cup Worcestershire sauce
1 (1.25-ounce) envelope French dip au jus mix

Place roast in roasting pan on a piece of extra heavy foil large enough to wrap entire roast. Douse roast generously with Worcestershire sauce on all sides. Seal meat in foil. Be sure foil is completely sealed all around. Bake at 300° for 4 hours on middle rack. Remove from oven. Allow to cool enough to handle. Slice or shred beef. Drain and measure beef broth. Add enough water to equal amount required on au jus packet. Pour broth and water into a small saucepan. Add seasoning packet. Prepare according to packet directions. Pour au jus over sliced or shredded beef. Place in freezer bag or container. For individual servings, spray a muffin tin with non-stick cooking spray. Fill muffin cups with meat and au jus. Cover and place pan in freezer just until frozen. Pop out and place in gallon freezer bag. Label and freeze. 12 servings.

To serve: Thaw roast and drain au jus. Heat roast and serve on warm sandwich rolls with bowls of au jus for dipping.

Oven Barbequed Beef

1 (3-pound) beef roast
1/4 cup Worcestershire sauce
1 cup ketchup
1/3 cup Worcestershire sauce

Place roast in roasting pan on a piece of extra heavy foil large enough to wrap entire roast. Douse roast with Worcestershire sauce (about 1/4 cup) on all sides. Seal meat in foil. Be sure foil is completely sealed all around. Bake at 300° for 4 hours. Remove from oven. Allow to cool enough to handle. Cut roast into 1 1/2-inch cubes. Arrange in shallow baking dish. Combine ketchup and 1/3 cup Worcestershire sauce. Bake at 350° for 1 hour. Allow to cool. Place in freezer bag or container. For individual servings, spray a muffin tin with non-stick cooking spray. Fill muffin cups with meat and sauce. Cover and place pan in freezer just until frozen. Pop out and place in gallon freezer bag. Label and freeze. 10 servings.

To serve: Thaw and heat. Serve on toasted buns.

To toast buns, split buns and spread with butter. Set oven to broil. Place buns, buttered side up, on baking sheet. Broil 4 inches from heat for 1 to 2 minutes, until golden brown. Watch carefully, they brown rapidly.

Cola Barbeque

1 (3 pound) beef roast
1 (24-ounce) bottle ketchup
1 (12-ounce) can of cola

Place roast in roasting pan on a piece of extra heavy foil large enough to wrap entire roast. Pour ketchup and cola over roast. Seal meat in foil. Be sure foil is completely sealed all around. Bake at 300° for 4 hours. Remove from oven. Allow to cool enough to handle. Slice or shred beef. Return meat to sauce and stir to coat. Allow to cool completely. Place in freezer bag or container. For individual servings, spray a muffin tin with non-stick cooking spray. Fill muffin cups with meat and sauce. Cover and place pan in freezer just until frozen. Pop out and place in gallon freezer bag. Label and freeze. 10 servings.

To serve: Thaw and heat. Serve on warm buns.

Texas Beef Brisket

1 (4-pound) whole beef brisket
2 teaspoons chili powder
2 teaspoons salt
1 teaspoon garlic powder
1 teaspoon onion powder
1 teaspoon pepper
1 teaspoon sugar
1 teaspoon ground mustard
1 (14.5-ounce) can beef broth
1 1/2 cups water

Trim brisket of all visible fat. Combine chili powder, salt, garlic, onion, pepper, sugar and ground mustard. Crush bay leaves and add to the mixture. Season brisket on all sides with mixture (you may not need to use all the seasoning mixture). Place brisket in roasting pan. Roast uncovered in 350° oven for 1 hour. Combine beef broth and water. Pour into roasting pan. Cover pan. Lower heat to 325°. Continue baking for 4 to 5 hours, basting every 30 minutes. Allow brisket to rest 15 minutes. Cut into thin slices across the grain. Allow to cool completely. Place in freezer bag with enough liquid moisten meat. Label and freeze. 12 servings.

To serve: Thaw and heat. Pile onto bulky buns. Top with sliced provolone. Broil just until cheese melts.

Roast Pork Hoagies

1 (3-pound) pork loin roast
1/2 cup soy sauce
1/2 cup beef broth
2 teaspoons minced garlic
1 tablespoon ground mustard
1 teaspoon minced ginger

Place pork roast in a baking pan. Combine soy sauce, beef broth, garlic, ground mustard and ginger. Pour mixture over roast. Turn several times to make sure roast is well coated. Cover tightly with extra heavy foil. Bake at 325° for 2 hours. Uncover and baste. Continue baking, uncovered for 1 hour, basting every 15 minutes. Allow to cool enough to handle. Shred or slice pork. Place meat and broth in freezer bag or container. For individual servings, spray a muffin tin with non-stick cooking spray. Fill muffin cups with meat and broth. Cover and place pan in freezer just until frozen. Pop out and place in gallon freezer bag. Label and freeze. 10 servings.

To serve: Thaw and heat. Pile onto hoagie rolls. Top with lettuce and tomato. Drizzle with **Italian Dressing** (page 264).

Reuben Sandwiches

1 (4-pound) corned beef brisket
1 tablespoon mixed whole pickling spices
1/2 cup sliced celery
1 cup chopped onion
1 cup sliced carrot
1/3 cup packed brown sugar
1 tablespoon mustard
1/2 cup sweet pickle juice

Place corned beef in a large pot. Cover with cold water and add pickling spices. Add celery, onion and carrot. Bring to a boil. Reduce heat and cover. Simmer for 4 1/2 hours. Cool corned beef in the broth. Remove beef and place in a shallow baking pan. Score top of meat. Mix brown sugar and mustard and rub over top of meat. Pour pickle juice in the pan. Bake at 300° for 1 hour, basting occasionally with pan drippings. Remove from oven and allow to cool enough to handle. Pull meat into chunks. Place in freezer bag with enough broth to moisten meat. For individual servings, spray a muffin tin with non-stick cooking spray. Pack muffin cups with meat. Spoon one tablespoon of broth into each. Cover and place pan in freezer just until frozen. Pop out and place in gallon freezer bag. Label and freeze. 12 servings.

To serve: Thaw and heat. Spread buns with **Simple Thousand Island Dressing** (page 269). Top with meat, Swiss cheese and sauerkraut.

Reuben Salad

1 recipe **Reuben Sandwiches** (page 106)
12 cups torn red curly leaf lettuce
1 1/2 cups sauerkraut
1 cups shredded Swiss cheese
1 onion
oil for deep-frying
Simple Thousand Island Dressing (page 269)

Prepare **Reuben Sandwich** filling as directed. Allow to cool completely. Place in freezer bag or container. To freeze filling for individual salad servings, spray cups of a muffin tin with non-stick cooking spray. Fill cups with filling. Press down gently. Cover and freeze. When frozen, pop out and place in a gallon freezer bag. Label and freeze. 6 servings.

To serve: Arrange lettuce on a serving platter (or in individual bowls). Heat **Reuben Sandwich** filling and mound onto salad. Mound sauerkraut beside meat. Top with shredded Swiss cheese. Cut onion into very thin slices. Cut slices in half and separate rings. Deep-fry in hot oil until golden. Mound onions over all. Serve with **Simple Thousand Island Dressing.**

BBQ Pork Sandwiches

3 tablespoons molasses
3 tablespoons ketchup
1 tablespoon Worcestershire sauce
1 teaspoon minced ginger
1/2 teaspoon grated lemon peel
1 teaspoon minced garlic
1 1/2 pounds pork tenderloin

In a medium bowl, combine molasses, ketchup, Worcestershire sauce, ginger, lemon peel, and garlic. Add pork, turning to coat. Cover tightly with extra heavy foil. Bake at 325° for 3 hours. Allow to cool enough to handle. Slice and return to sauce. Allow to cool completely. Place in freezer bag or container. For individual servings, spray a muffin tin with non-stick cooking spray. Fill muffin cups with meat and sauce. Cover and place pan in freezer just until frozen. Pop out and place in gallon freezer bag. Label and freeze. 6 servings.

To serve: Thaw and heat. Spoon pork slices and sauce on soft dinner rolls. Top with cole slaw.

Minced ginger and garlic can be found in small jars in the produce section of the grocery store, usually beside the fresh ginger and garlic.

BBQ Pork Salad

1 recipe **BBQ Pork Sandwiches** (page 108)
6 cups torn Iceberg lettuce
6 cups torn red curly leaf lettuce
1/2 cup shredded Cheddar cheese
1/2 cup shredded Monterey Jack cheese
1 cup toasted French fried onions
Honey Mustard Dressing (page 266)

Prepare **BBQ Pork** as directed. Allow to cool completely. Place in freezer bag or container. To freeze filling for individual salad servings, spray cups of a muffin tin with non-stick cooking spray. Fill cups with filling. Press down gently. Cover and freeze. When frozen, pop out and place in a gallon freezer bag. Label and freeze. 6 servings.

To serve: Arrange Iceberg and red curly leaf lettuce in a large salad bowl (or in individual bowls). Heat **BBQ Pork** and mound onto lettuce. Top with shredded Cheddar and Monterey Jack cheeses. Sprinkle toasted French fried onions over all. Serve with **Honey Mustard Dressing**.

To toast French fried onions, arrange onions in a single layer on a shallow baking sheet. Place under broiler for about 30 seconds, until golden and sizzling.

Apple Roast Pork Sandwiches

1 (4-pound) pork roast
1/3 cup Worcestershire sauce
3/4 cup packed brown sugar
1 cup apple juice
1/2 teaspoon salt

Place roast in dish or pan barely larger than roast. Douse roast on all sides with Worcestershire sauce. Press brown sugar on sides and top of roast. Pour apple juice into the pan baking pan but not over roast. Cover tightly with extra heavy foil and lid. Place roast in pre-heated 400° oven. Immediately reduce heat to 275°. Bake for 5 hours. Remove and allow to cool enough to handle. Meat should pull apart easily. Shred meat and sprinkle with salt. Place meat and broth in freezer bag or container. For individual servings, spray a muffin tin with non-stick cooking spray. Fill muffin cups with meat and broth. Cover and place pan in freezer just until frozen. Pop out and place in gallon freezer bag. Label and freeze. 12 servings.

To serve: Thaw and heat. Spoon onto warm onion rolls. Serve with sliced apples or applesauce.

Apple Roast Pork Salad

1 recipe **Apple Roast Pork Sandwiches** (page 110)
6 cups torn Iceberg lettuce
6 cups baby spinach leaves
1 cup sliced apple
1 cup sliced Cheddar cheese
Poppy Seed Dressing (page 268)

Prepare **Apple Roast Pork Sandwich** filling as directed. Allow to cool completely. Place in freezer bag or container. To freeze filling for individual salad servings, spray cups of a muffin tin with non-stick cooking spray. Fill cups with filling. Press down gently. Cover and freeze. When frozen, pop out and place in a gallon freezer bag. Label and freeze. 6 servings.

To serve: Arrange lettuce in a large salad bowl (or in individual bowls). Heat **Apple Roast Pork** filling and mound onto lettuce. Top with sliced apple and sliced Cheddar cheese. Serve with **Poppy Seed Dressing**.

Chinese Pork Sandwiches

1 (3-pound) pork tenderloin
1/2 cup prune juice
1/4 cup soy sauce
3/4 cup ketchup
1/2 cup sugar

Trim pork tenderloin and pierce on all sides with a fork. Place in a baking pan. Combine prune juice, soy sauce, ketchup and sugar. Pour over pork. Turn several times to coat pork. Bake covered at 350° for 1 hour. Uncover and bake for 45 minutes, basting with sauce every 15 minutes. Remove from oven and allow to cool completely. Place whole pork tenderloin and sauce in a freezer bag. For individual servings, slice pork and place in cups of a muffin tin. Spoon sauce over sliced pork. Cover and place pan in freezer just until frozen. Pop out and place in gallon freezer bag. Label and freeze. 10 servings.

To serve: Thaw and heat. Spoon sliced pork and sauce onto crusty rolls. Top with sliced red and green bell peppers and Monterey Jack cheese. Broil just until cheese is melted.

Chinese Pork Salad

1 recipe **Chinese Pork Sandwiches** (page 112)
12 cups torn curly leaf lettuce
1 cup sliced celery
1 (8-ounce) can sliced water chestnuts
1 cup chow mein noodles
Chinese Salad Dressing (page 271)

Prepare **Chinese Pork Sandwich** filling as directed. Allow to cool completely. Place in freezer bag or container. To freeze filling for individual salad servings, spray cups of a muffin tin with non-stick cooking spray. Fill cups with filling. Press down gently. Cover and freeze. When frozen, pop out and place in a gallon freezer bag. Label and freeze. 6 servings.

To serve: Arrange lettuce in a large salad bowl (or in individual bowls). Heat **Chinese Pork** filling and mound on to lettuce. Top with sliced celery and drained water chestnuts. Toss gently. Top with chow mein noodles. Serve with **Chinese Salad Dressing.**

Chow mein noodles are especially delicious on salad if they have been toasted. Arrange chow mein noodles in a thin layer on a shallow baking sheet. Broil for about 30 seconds until golden and sizzling.

Barbeque Franks

1 (16-ounce) package hot dogs
1 1/2 tablespoons Worcestershire sauce
1/4 cup apple cider vinegar
2 tablespoons sugar
1/2 cup ketchup
1/2 cup water
1/2 cup chopped onion
1/2 cup chopped green bell pepper

Place hot dogs in a greased baking dish. Combine Worcestershire sauce, vinegar and sugar. Stir in ketchup, water, onion and green bell pepper. Pour over hot dogs. Bake at 350° for 1 hour. Allow to cool completely. Place in freezer bag or container. For individual servings, spray a muffin tin with non-stick cooking spray. Cut hot dogs in half and place two halves in each muffin cup. Divide sauce among the cups. Cover and place pan in freezer just until frozen. Pop out and place in gallon freezer bag. Label and freeze. 8 servings.

To serve: Thaw and heat. Spoon into hot dog buns. Serve alone or with shredded lettuce and cheese.

Parmesan Chicken Cordon Bleu

4 small boneless skinless chicken breast halves
4 ham slices
4 Swiss cheese slices
4 teaspoons mustard
1 cup flour
1/2 teaspoon salt
1/8 teaspoon pepper
1 egg
1 tablespoon water
1 cup dry bread crumbs
1/3 cup canned Parmesan cheese
8 teaspoons butter

Butterfly each chicken breast half horizontally. (Do not cut all the way through since you will want to fill the breasts and then fold them back together.) Place ham slice and cheese slice onto each butterflied chicken breast half. Spread each with a teaspoon of mustard. Fold the chicken back together. Push in any ham or cheese that sticks out. Use toothpicks to keep the edges together if necessary. Combine flour, salt and pepper in one bowl. Combine egg and water in a second bowl. Combine bread crumbs and Parmesan cheese in a third bowl. Dip each filled breast into flour mixture first, then into the egg mixture and finally into the crumb and cheese mixture. Place into a generously greased baking dish, not close enough to touch. Top each with a teaspoon of butter. Bake at 350° for 20 minutes. Turn and top each with a teaspoon of butter. Bake an additional 20 minutes. Allow to cool completely. Wrap separately in plastic. Place together in a freezer bag. Label and freeze. 4 servings.

To serve: Thaw and heat in microwave, oven or toaster oven.

Oven Fried Chicken

3 pounds chicken pieces
2 (1-ounce) envelopes Italian dressing mix
3 tablespoons flour
2 teaspoons salt
1/4 cup lemon juice
3/4 cup milk
1 1/2 cups complete pancake mix
1 teaspoon paprika
1/2 teaspoon salt
1/4 teaspoon pepper
oil for cooking

Combine Italian dressing mix, flour, salt and lemon juice to make a paste. Coat chicken pieces evenly. Place chicken pieces in a bowl. Cover and refrigerate for several hours or overnight. Place milk in a small bowl. In a separate bowl, combine pancake mix, paprika, salt and pepper. Dip chicken pieces in milk, then into the pancake coating. Dust off excess. In a shallow skillet, heat 1/2-inch oil. Brown chicken pieces for about 4 minutes per side. Remove and place in a single layer in a shallow baking pan. Cover tightly with extra heavy foil. Bake at 350° for 1 hour. Uncover and baste with milk. Return to oven uncovered and bake at 400° for 15 minutes. Allow to cool completely. Place in a single layer on a baking sheet and cover with plastic. Place in freezer just until frozen. Place frozen chicken in a freezer bag. Label and freeze. 6 servings.

To serve: Thaw and heat in microwave, oven or in toaster oven.

Oven Fried Drumsticks

1/4 cup flour
1 egg
1/4 cup milk
1 cup corn flake crumbs
1/2 teaspoon garlic powder
1/2 teaspoon onion powder
1/2 teaspoon paprika
1/2 teaspoon salt
1/4 teaspoon pepper
8 chicken drumsticks

Place flour in a shallow dish. Beat egg and milk in a second dish. In a third dish, combine corn flake crumbs with garlic powder, onion powder, paprika, salt and pepper. Dip chicken in the flour, then into the egg mixture, then into the cereal mixture. Arrange chicken on a greased baking sheet. Bake at 375° for 25 minutes. Turn and bake an additional 25 minutes. Chicken should be cooked through and golden. Remove from oven and allow to cool completely. Cover with plastic and place pan of chicken in freezer. Transfer frozen chicken pieces to freezer bag. Label and freeze. 8 pieces.

To serve: Thaw and heat in microwave, oven or in toaster oven.

Garlic Ginger Chicken Sandwiches

2 large boneless skinless chicken breast halves
3 teaspoons minced garlic
3 tablespoons ground ginger
1 tablespoon olive oil
1/2 cup fresh lime juice

Butterfly chicken by cutting through thickest part of chicken and laying open. Pound with a meat mallet to flatten to near equal thickness. Cut into 4 portions. Combine garlic, ginger, oil and lime juice. Mix well. Place in a large resealable bag. Add chicken and seal bag. Turn to coat. Place in refrigerator. Allow chicken to marinate for about 20 minutes. Remove chicken from bag and broil for about 7 minutes. Turn and baste with marinade. Broil for additional 7 minutes or until chicken is cooked through. Allow to cool completely. Place in freezer bag or container. For individual servings, place cooked chicken on a baking sheet. Cover with plastic wrap and place in freezer just until frozen. Transfer frozen chicken to a freezer bag. Label and freeze. 4 servings.

To serve: Thaw and heat. Place chicken on soft rolls and top with provolone cheese. Broil until cheese melts. Top with lettuce, tomato and a squeeze of lime juice.

Ranch Chicken Sandwiches

2 boneless skinless chicken breast halves
1 (1-ounce) envelope Ranch dressing mix
2 tablespoons olive oil
1 tablespoon red wine vinegar

Butterfly chicken by cutting through thickest part of chicken and laying open. Pound with a meat mallet to flatten to near equal thickness. Cut into 4 portions. Combine dressing mix, olive oil and red wine vinegar. Place in large resealable bag. Add chicken. Seal and shake to coat meat thoroughly, pressing mixture into meat. Refrigerate and marinate for at least 1 hour. Remove chicken from bag and place in a greased baking dish. Bake at 350° for about 20 minutes or until chicken is cooked through. Remove from oven and allow to cool completely. Place in freezer bag or container. For individual servings, place cooked chicken on a baking sheet. Cover with plastic wrap and place in freezer just until frozen. Transfer frozen chicken to a freezer bag. Label and freeze. 4 servings.

To serve: Thaw and heat. Place chicken on soft rolls and top with provolone cheese. Broil until cheese melts. Top with lettuce and tomato. Drizzle with **Ranch Dressing** (page 263).

Teriyaki Chicken Sandwiches

4 small boneless skinless chicken breast halves
1/3 cup peanut oil
1/3 cup soy sauce
3 tablespoons honey
1 tablespoon red wine vinegar
1 teaspoon minced garlic
1 teaspoon ground ginger
1/4 teaspoon pepper

Place chicken in a resealable bag. Combine oil, soy sauce, honey, vinegar, garlic, ginger and pepper. Pour over chicken in bag. Seal and turn to coat. Place in refrigerator and allow to marinate for 30 minutes. Remove chicken from bag and place in a greased baking dish. Bake chicken at 350° for 20 minutes or until cooked through. Meanwhile, pour marinade in a saucepan. Boil until liquid is reduced by half. Remove chicken from oven and allow to cool completely. Place chicken and sauce in freezer bag or container. For individual servings, place each piece in a separate small sandwich bag with a small amount of sauce. Place individual bags into a larger freezer bag. Label and freeze. 4 servings.

To serve: Thaw and heat. Cut chicken into 1/2-inch slices. Arrange sliced chicken and sauce on buns. Top with sliced Mozzarella cheese and sliced pineapple. Broil until cheese melts.

Maple Teriyaki Chicken Sandwiches

1/4 cup soy sauce
1 cup water
1/3 cup **Maple Syrup** (page 285)
3 tablespoons sesame oil
2 teaspoons minced garlic
1 tablespoon minced ginger
2 teaspoon black pepper
10 chicken tenders
2 tablespoons cornstarch

Combine soy sauce, water, maple syrup, sesame oil, garlic, ginger and pepper. Place in resealable bag. Add chicken. Seal bag and turn to coat. Place in refrigerator and allow chicken to marinate for 2 hours. Remove chicken and place in a greased baking dish. Bake at 350° for about 20 minutes, until chicken is cooked through. Meanwhile, pour marinade into a small saucepan. Add cornstarch and whisk until smooth. Heat marinade to boiling. Cook and stir until thickened. Pour thickened marinade over cooked chicken. Turn to coat. Place under broiler for 3 minutes. Turn and broil an additional 3 minutes. Remove from oven and allow to cool completely. Place in freezer bag or container. For individual servings, place each piece in a separate small sandwich bag with a small amount of sauce. Place individual bags into a larger freezer bag. Label and freeze. 10 servings.

To serve: Thaw and heat. Place chicken tenders and sauce in toasted hot dog buns. Top with lettuce and tomato.

For **Maple Teriyaki Chicken Bowls**, cut chicken in 1-inch cubes. Pour thickened sauce over all. Place rice in single serving-sized freezer containers. Top with chicken. Label and freeze.

Pineapple Teriyaki Chicken Sandwiches

10 chicken tenders
1/3 cup pineapple juice
1/4 cup teriyaki sauce
2 teaspoons honey
2 teaspoons packed brown sugar
2 teaspoons butter
1 teaspoon peanut oil
1 teaspoon cornstarch

Place chicken in a greased baking dish. Combine pineapple juice, teriyaki sauce, honey and brown sugar. Pour over chicken. Cover with plastic and refrigerate for 2 hours. Remove chicken. Pour marinade into a saucepan. In a skillet, melt 1 teaspoon butter and add the oil. Brown chicken in oil and butter. Place in baking dish. Combine reserved marinade and cornstarch. Add remaining 1 teaspoon butter. Heat to boiling. Cook and stir until slightly thickened. Pour over chicken. Cover with lid or foil. Bake at 350° for 25 minutes. Turn and bake 20 minutes longer. Remove from oven and allow to cool completely. Place in freezer bag or container. For individual servings, place each piece in a separate small sandwich bag with a small amount of sauce. Place individual bags into a larger freezer bag. Label and freeze. 10 servings.

To serve: Thaw and heat. Place chicken tenders and sauce in toasted hot dog buns. For each sandwich cut one pineapple ring in half. Place two halves in each bun.

Pineapple Teriyaki Chicken is delicious served as salad. Top salad greens with chicken and drained pineapple tidbits.

Honey Mustard Chicken Sandwiches

2 large boneless skinless chicken breast halves
1 cup honey
1 cup spicy mustard
2 tablespoons mayonnaise
1 tablespoon barbeque sauce

Butterfly chicken by cutting through thickest part of chicken and laying open. Pound with a meat mallet to flatten to near equal thickness. Cut into 4 portions. Bake at 350° for 20 minutes. Pour off liquid. Combine honey, mustard, mayonnaise and barbeque sauce. Pour over chicken. Bake 25 minutes. Allow to cool. Place in freezer bag or container. For individual servings, place each piece in a separate small sandwich bag with a small amount of sauce. Place individual bags into a larger freezer bag. Label and freeze. 4 servings.

To serve: Thaw and heat. Place chicken and sauce in toasted bun. Top with lettuce and tomato.

For **Honey Mustard Chicken Bowls**, cut chicken in 1-inch cubes. Bake in sauce. Place rice in single serving-sized freezer containers. Top with chicken and sauce. Label and freeze.

BBQ Chicken Sandwiches

2 large boneless skinless chicken breast halves
1/2 cup ketchup
1/2 cup packed brown sugar
1 tablespoon mustard
1 tablespoon Worcestershire sauce
1 tablespoon apple cider vinegar
1/4 cup water

Butterfly chicken by cutting through thickest part of chicken and laying open. Pound with a meat mallet to flatten to near equal thickness. Cut into 4 portions. Bake at 350° for 20 minutes. Pour off liquid. In a saucepan, combine ketchup, brown sugar, mustard, Worcestershire sauce, vinegar and water. Boil until sauce is thick. Pour over chicken. Bake 20 minutes. Allow to cool. Place in freezer bag or container. For individual servings, place each piece in a separate small sandwich bag with a small amount of sauce. Place individual bags into a larger freezer bag. Label and freeze. 4 servings.

To serve: Thaw and heat. Place chicken and sauce on sandwich rolls. Top with Monterey Jack cheese and shredded lettuce.

Golden Chicken Wings

2/3 cup dry bread crumbs
1 teaspoon onion powder
1/2 teaspoon garlic salt
1/2 teaspoon paprika
1 egg
1 tablespoon milk
10 chicken wings

In a bowl, combine dry bread crumbs, onion powder, garlic salt and paprika. In a separate bowl, whisk together egg and milk. Cut each chicken wing into 3 sections. Discard wing tips. Dip wing sections in egg and then crumbs. Place in a single layer on a greased 15 x 10 x 1-inch baking pan. Bake uncovered at 425° for 20 minutes. Turn and bake for an additional 15 minutes. Allow to cool. Place wings in a freezer bag. Label and freeze. 20 pieces.

To serve: Thaw and heat.

Maple Chicken Wings

1/4 cup **Maple Syrup** (page 285)
1/4 cup chili sauce
1 tablespoon soy sauce
1/2 teaspoon ground mustard
dash cayenne pepper
12 chicken wings

Combine maple syrup, chili sauce, soy sauce, ground mustard and cayenne pepper. Separate chicken wings into 3 sections. Discard wing tips. Place wing sections into sauce. Turn to coat. Pour into an ungreased 15 x 10 x 1-inch baking pan, placing wings in a single layer. Bake uncovered at 375° for 45 to 55 minutes, turning once and brushing with sauce after 30 minutes. Allow to cool. Place chicken and sauce in freezer bag. Label and freeze. 24 pieces.

To serve: Thaw and heat. Serve chicken with sauce.

Taco Wings

1/2 cup flour
1 (1.25-ounce) envelope taco seasoning
1 tablespoon canola oil
12 chicken wings

In shallow dish, combine flour and taco seasoning. Mix well. Stir in oil with a fork. Cut each wing into 3 pieces. Discard wing tips. Coat wing sections with flour mixture. Coat again to use up flour mixture. Place on baking sheet that has been sprayed with nonstick cooking spray. Bake at 350° for 25 minutes. Turn and bake an additional 20 minutes. Allow to cool completely. Freeze in a single layer on baking sheet. When frozen, transfer to gallon freezer bag. Label and return to freezer. 24 pieces.

To serve: Thaw and heat. Serve with **Green Chile Ranch Sauce** (page 276) for dipping.

Stove Top Recipes

Sloppy Joes

1 pound lean ground beef
1/2 cup chopped onion
1 cup chopped celery
1/4 cup ketchup
2 tablespoons packed brown sugar
1 tablespoon mustard
1 tablespoon Worcestershire sauce
1 teaspoon salt
1/8 teaspoon pepper

In a large skillet, brown ground beef with onion and celery. Stir in ketchup, brown sugar, mustard, Worcestershire sauce, salt and pepper. Partially cover and simmer for about 30 minutes, stirring occasionally. Allow to cool completely. Place in freezer bag or container. For individual servings, spray cups of a muffin tin with non-stick cooking spray. Pack muffin cups with filling. Cover and place pan in freezer just until frozen. Pop out and place in gallon freezer bag. Label and freeze. 8 servings.

To serve: Thaw and heat. Serve on hamburger buns.

 For simple variety, serve **Sloppy Joes** on hot dog buns. Fun and easier to eat, too!

Quick Sloppy Joes

1 pound lean ground beef
1 teaspoon onion powder
1 1/2 teaspoons garlic salt
1/8 teaspoon pepper
1/3 cup chili sauce
1/4 cup packed brown sugar
1 tablespoon apple cider vinegar
1 tablespoon mustard
1 (8-ounce) can tomato sauce

Brown ground beef with onion, garlic salt and pepper. Stir in chili sauce, brown sugar, vinegar, mustard and tomato sauce. Bring to a boil. Reduce heat. Simmer, uncovered, for about 10 minutes. Allow to cool completely. Place in freezer bag or container. For individual servings, spray cups of a muffin tin with non-stick cooking spray. Pack muffin cups with filling. Cover and place pan in freezer just until frozen. Pop out and place in gallon freezer bag. Label and freeze. 8 servings.

To serve: Thaw and heat. Serve on toasted hamburger buns.

To toast hamburger buns, split buns and spread cut side with butter. Place on 350° hot griddle until golden brown.

Sloppy Lani

1 1/2 pounds lean ground beef
1 (10.75-ounce) can tomato soup
1/2 cup ketchup
2 tablespoons apple cider vinegar
1 tablespoon ground mustard
2 tablespoons Worcestershire sauce
1 tablespoon packed brown sugar
1 teaspoon salt
1/4 teaspoon pepper

Brown ground beef. Stir in tomato soup, ketchup and vinegar. Mix well. Add ground mustard, Worcestershire sauce, brown sugar, salt and pepper. Stir and simmer for 30 minutes. Allow to cool completely. Place in freezer bag or container. For individual servings, spray a muffin tin with non-stick cooking spray. Spoon about 3 tablespoons into each muffin cup. Cover and place pan in freezer just until frozen. Pop out and place in gallon freezer bag. Label and freeze. 12 servings.

To serve: Thaw and heat. For each serving, cover one flour tortilla with shredded Cheddar cheese. Spoon meat filling over one half of the tortilla. Microwave on a paper plate until cheese is melted. Fold cheese side over meat side of tortilla. Press together. Cut in wedges with a pizza cutter.

This delicious recipe is named after the author's daughter, Lani, who invented it. Try substituting **Tomato Beef Taco** filling (page 246).

Sloppy Jacks

1 pound lean ground beef
1/2 cup chopped onion
1 teaspoon minced garlic
1 cup cooked pumpkin
1 cup tomato sauce
2 tablespoons mustard
2 tablespoons packed brown sugar
2 teaspoons chili powder
1/2 teaspoon salt

Brown ground beef with onion and garlic. Stir in cooked pumpkin, tomato sauce, mustard, brown sugar, chili powder and salt. Heat until bubbly. Reduce heat. Cover and simmer for 10 minutes. Allow to cool completely. Place in freezer bag or container. For individual servings, spray cups of a muffin tin with non-stick cooking spray. Pack muffin cups with filling. Cover and place pan in freezer just until frozen. Pop out and place in gallon freezer bag. Label and freeze. 8 servings.

To serve: Thaw and heat. Serve on buns. Decorate with American cheese cut into Jack-o-lantern face shapes. Replace bun top just before eating.

Sloppy Josés

1 pound lean ground beef
1/2 cup chopped onion
1/2 cup chopped green bell pepper
1 (4-ounce) can diced green chiles
1 teaspoon minced garlic
1 tablespoon chili powder
1/2 teaspoon salt
1 tablespoon sugar
1 (8-ounce) can tomato sauce
1 cup tomato juice
1 (15-ounce) can pinto beans, drained

Brown ground beef with onion, green pepper, green chiles and garlic until beef is no longer pink. Stir often while cooking to break meat into small pieces. Add chili powder, salt and sugar. Cook and mix well. Stir in tomato sauce and tomato juice. Bring to a boil. Reduce heat. Cover partially and simmer, stirring often, for about 20 minutes. Remove from heat and add drained beans. Allow to cool completely. Place in freezer bag or container. For individual servings, spray cups of a muffin tin with non-stick cooking spray. Pack muffin cups with filling. Cover and place pan in freezer just until frozen. Pop out and place in gallon freezer bag. Label and freeze. 10 servings.

To serve: Thaw and heat. Serve on buns. Top with shredded Cheddar cheese.

Sloppy Giuseppes

1 pound lean ground beef
1/2 pound hot Italian sausage
1/2 cup chopped onion
1/2 cup chopped green bell pepper
1 cup sliced mushrooms
1 teaspoon minced garlic
1 (8-ounce) can tomato sauce
1 (6-ounce) can tomato paste
1 cup water
1 teaspoon salt
1/2 teaspoon oregano
1 teaspoon sugar

Brown ground beef and sausage with onion, green pepper, mushrooms and garlic until meat is no longer pink. Stir often while cooking to break meat into small pieces. Stir in tomato sauce, tomato paste, water, salt, oregano and sugar. Bring to a boil. Reduce heat. Cover partially and simmer, stirring often, for about 20 minutes. Allow to cool completely. Place in freezer bag or container. For individual servings, spray cups of a muffin tin with non-stick cooking spray. Pack muffin cups with filling. Cover and place pan in freezer just until frozen. Pop out and place in gallon freezer bag. Label and freeze. 10 servings.

To serve: Thaw and heat. Serve on toasted Italian rolls. Top with shredded fresh Parmesan cheese.

 For milder **Sloppy Giuseppes**, substitute mild Italian sausage for the hot Italian sausage.

Pizza Joes

1 pound lean ground beef
1/2 pound hot Italian sausage
1/2 cup chopped onion
1/2 cup chopped green bell pepper
1 cup sliced mushrooms
1 teaspoon minced garlic
1 (2-ounce) package sliced pepperoni
1 (2.25-ounce) can sliced black olives
1 cup spaghetti sauce
1 teaspoon sugar

Brown ground beef and sausage with onion, green pepper, mushrooms and garlic until meat is no longer pink. Stir often while cooking to break meat into small pieces. Cut pepperoni slices in half. Stir in pepperoni, drained black olives, spaghetti sauce and sugar. Bring to a boil. Reduce heat. Cover partially and simmer, stirring often, for about 20 minutes. Allow to cool completely. Place in freezer bag or container. For individual servings, spray cups of a muffin tin with non-stick cooking spray. Pack muffin cups with filling. Cover and place pan in freezer just until frozen. Pop out and place in gallon freezer bag. Label and freeze. 10 servings.

To serve: Thaw and heat. Serve on buns. Top with generous portion of shredded Mozzarella cheese. Broil briefly, until cheese is melted.

Pizza Joe Salad

1 recipe **Pizza Joes** (page 136)
12 cups torn Iceberg lettuce
1 (2.25-ounce) can sliced black olives, drained
1/2 cup sliced mushrooms
1 cup shredded fresh Parmesan cheese
Italian Dressing (page 264)

Prepare **Pizzas Joes** as directed. Allow to cool completely. Place in freezer bag or container. To freeze filling for individual salad servings, spray cups of a muffin tin with non-stick cooking spray. Fill cups with filling. Press down gently. Cover and place pan in freezer just until frozen. Pop out and place in gallon freezer bag. Label and freeze. 6 servings.

To serve: Arrange lettuce in a large salad bowl (or in individual bowls). Heat **Sloppy Joe** filling place on lettuce. Add black olives and sliced mushrooms. Top with shredded fresh Parmesan cheese. Serve with **Italian Dressing.**

For salad variations, substitute **Sloppy Giuseppes** (page 135) or **Mushroom Pizza Buns** (page 140) for the **Pizza Joes.**

Chalupa Joes

1 pound lean ground beef
1 cup picante sauce
1 teaspoon mustard
1 tablespoon packed brown sugar
2 tablespoons soy sauce
1/2 teaspoon lemon pepper
1/4 teaspoon garlic salt

Brown ground beef. Add picante sauce, mustard, brown sugar, soy sauce, lemon pepper and garlic salt. Simmer uncovered for 10 minutes. Allow to cool completely. Place in freezer bag or container. For individual servings, spray cups of a muffin tin with non-stick cooking spray. Pack muffin cups with filling. Cover and place pan in freezer just until frozen. Pop out and place in gallon freezer bag. Label and freeze. 8 servings.

To serve: Thaw and heat. Spoon onto buns. Top with chopped onion. Serve with refried beans, tortilla chips and salsa.

 Chalupa Joes are also delicious served on warm flour tortillas.

Smoky Barbeque Beef Sandwiches

2 1/2 pounds lean ground beef
1 cup water
3/4 cup corn syrup
1 (6-ounce) can tomato paste
2/3 cup apple cider vinegar
1/3 cup packed dark brown sugar
3 tablespoons molasses
1 1/4 teaspoons liquid smoke
1 teaspoon salt
1/4 teaspoon onion powder
1/4 teaspoon pepper
1/4 teaspoon ground mustard
1/8 teaspoon garlic powder
dash cayenne pepper

Brown ground beef, stirring frequently to break into small pieces. In a saucepan, combine water, corn syrup, tomato paste, vinegar and brown sugar. Stir until sugar is dissolved. Stir in molasses, liquid smoke, salt, onion powder, pepper, mustard, garlic powder and cayenne pepper. Whisk until smooth. Bring to a boil. Reduce heat. Simmer uncovered for 45 minutes or until thick. Pour over browned ground beef. Simmer 10 minutes. Allow to cool completely. Place in freezer bag or container. For individual servings, spray cups of a muffin tin with non-stick cooking spray. Pack muffin cups with filling. Cover and place pan in freezer just until frozen. Pop out and place in gallon freezer bag. Label and freeze. 16 servings.

To serve: Thaw and heat. Serve on buns.

Mushroom Pizza Buns

2 pounds lean ground beef
1 cup chopped onion
1 cup sliced mushrooms
1 teaspoon minced garlic
1 cup ketchup
1 tablespoon Worcestershire sauce
1 tablespoon packed brown sugar
1/2 teaspoon Italian seasoning
1/4 teaspoon ground mustard

Brown ground beef with onion, mushrooms and garlic. Stir in ketchup, Worcestershire sauce, brown sugar, Italian seasoning and ground mustard. Reduce heat. Cover and simmer for 20 minutes. Allow to cool completely. Place in freezer bag or container. For individual servings, spray cups of a muffin tin with non-stick cooking spray. Pack muffin cups with filling. Cover and place pan in freezer just until frozen. Pop out and place in gallon freezer bag. Label and freeze. 12 servings.

To serve: Thaw and heat. Serve on toasted hamburger buns. Top with Mozzarella cheese. Broil briefly, until cheese is melted.

Pennsylvania BBQ

2 pounds lean ground beef
1 cup chopped onion
1/2 cup chopped green bell pepper
1/4 cup chopped celery
3 (8-ounce) cans tomato sauce
1/2 cup ketchup
1 tablespoon Worcestershire sauce
2 tablespoons apple cider vinegar
2 tablespoons packed brown sugar
2 teaspoons salt
1/2 teaspoon pepper

Brown ground beef with onion, bell pepper and celery. Stir in tomato sauce, ketchup, Worcestershire sauce, vinegar, brown sugar, salt and pepper. Cook and stir until bubbly. Reduce heat. Cover and simmer, stirring occasionally, for about 1 hour. Allow to cool completely. Place in freezer bag or container. For individual servings, spray cups of a muffin tin with non-stick cooking spray. Pack muffin cups with filling. Cover and place pan in freezer just until frozen. Pop out and place in gallon freezer bag. Label and freeze. 12 servings.

To serve: Thaw and heat. Serve on buns.

Island Beef

1 1/2 pounds lean ground beef
2/3 cup chopped onion
1/2 chopped green bell pepper
1/2 cup shredded carrots
1 cup crushed pineapple
1 cup ketchup
2 tablespoons soy sauce
1 tablespoon white vinegar
1/2 teaspoon minced ginger
1 tablespoon cornstarch
1/2 cup beef broth

Brown ground beef with onion, bell pepper and carrots. Stir in pineapple, ketchup, soy sauce, vinegar and ginger. Dissolve cornstarch in beef broth and add to beef mixture. Simmer gently for 20 minutes. Allow to cool completely. Place in freezer bag or container. For individual servings, spray cups of a muffin tin with non-stick cooking spray. Pack muffin cups with filling. Cover and place pan in freezer just until frozen. Pop out and place in gallon freezer bag. Label and freeze. 12 servings.

To serve: Thaw and heat. Serve on buns.

Island Beef Salad

1 recipe **Island Beef** (page 142)
6 cups torn Iceberg lettuce
6 cups torn Romaine lettuce
1 (8-ounce) can pineapple tidbits
1 (8-ounce) can Mandarin orange segments
square wonton wraps
oil for deep-frying
Ranch Dressing (page 263)

Prepare **Island Beef** as directed. Allow to cool completely. Place in freezer bag or container. To freeze filling for individual salad servings, spray cups of a muffin tin with non-stick cooking spray. Fill cups with filling. Press down gently. Cover and place pan in freezer just until frozen. Pop out and place in gallon freezer bag. Label and freeze. 6 servings.

To serve: Arrange lettuce in a large salad bowl (or in individual bowls). Heat **Island Beef** and place on lettuce. Add drained pineapple tidbits and drained Mandarin orange segments. Stack several wonton wraps. Cut through entire stack at once into very thin strips. Deep-fry in hot oil until golden and crispy. Pile on top of salad. Serve with **Ranch Dressing**.

Meatball Heroes

1/2 cup fresh bread crumbs
1/4 cup milk
1 egg
1 teaspoon Italian seasoning
1/4 teaspoon salt
1/4 teaspoon crushed red pepper flakes
1 pound lean ground beef
3/4 pound ground pork
1/4 cup canola oil
1/2 cup chopped onion
1 teaspoon minced garlic
1 (28-ounce) can Italian tomatoes
1 cup tomato sauce
1 1/2 teaspoons Italian seasoning
1/4 teaspoon crushed red pepper flakes

Combine fresh bread crumbs, milk, egg, Italian seasoning, salt and red pepper flakes. Mix in ground beef and ground pork. Using about 1 tablespoon for each, form mixture into meatballs. Cook meatballs in hot oil until browned on all sides. Meatballs do not need to be cooked all the way through. Remove meatballs and set aside. Remove all but about 2 tablespoons drippings from skillet. Add onion and garlic and cook until soft. Add tomatoes, tomato sauce, Italian seasoning and red pepper flakes. Reduce heat, partially cover and simmer for 30 minutes. Return meatballs to skillet and cook, uncovered, for 15 minutes. Allow to cool completely. Spray a muffin tin with non-stick cooking spray. Place 3 meatballs in each of 6 muffin cups. Add to each cup about 1/4 cup sauce. Divide the remaining sauce among the other 6 cups. Cover and freeze. Pop out "cubes" and place in freezer bag. Label and freeze. 6 servings.

To serve: For each Hero, thaw and heat one meatball "cube" and one sauce "cube". Pull out soft insides of Italian roll, leaving shells about 3/4-inch thick. Place 3 meatballs in bottom of each roll and spoon sauce over top. Top with shredded fresh Parmesan cheese and the top of the roll. Serve with the additional sauce.

Pizza Potatoes

1 pound lean ground beef
1 cup chopped green bell pepper
1 cup chopped onion
1 cup sliced mushrooms
1/2 teaspoon salt
1/8 teaspoon pepper
1 (2.25-ounce) can sliced black olives
1 (14.5-ounce) can Italian tomatoes
1 cup spaghetti sauce
1/2 teaspoon sugar

Brown ground beef with bell pepper, onion, mushrooms, salt and pepper. Stir in drained black olives, undrained tomatoes, spaghetti sauce and sugar. Simmer for 20 minutes. Remove from heat. Allow to cool completely. Place in freezer bag or container. For individual servings, spray a muffin tin with non-stick cooking spray. Pack filling into muffin cups. Cover and place pan in freezer just until frozen. Pop out and place in gallon freezer bag. Label and freeze. 8 servings.

To serve: Thaw and heat. For each serving, slice the top off of a hot baked potato and fluff pulp with a fork. Spoon meat sauce onto potato. Top with shredded Mozzarella cheese. Drizzle with **Ranch Dressing** (page 263).

Fiesta Slices

1 pound lean ground beef
1 pound pork sausage
1/2 cup chopped onion
1 pound Mexican-style processed American cheese
1 tablespoon Worcestershire sauce
1/2 teaspoon salt
1/8 teaspoon pepper
1 (1-pound) loaf sliced snack rye bread

Brown ground beef and sausage with onion. Cut cheese into cubes. Stir in cheese, Worcestershire sauce, salt and pepper. Heat and stir until cheese is melted and smooth. Spoon 1 heaping tablespoon of meat mixture on each slice of bread. Arrange in a single layer on baking sheet. Cover and place in freezer just until frozen. Transfer frozen slices to a gallon freezer bag. Label and freeze. 45 slices.

To serve: Broil 4 inches from heat until cheese is bubbly and just starts to brown.

 Substitute any loaf of sliced snack size bread for the rye bread.

Teriyaki Steak Bowls

2 pounds beef sirloin steak
2 tablespoons canola oil
1 tablespoon cornstarch
1 tablespoon cold water
1/2 cup sugar
1/3 cup soy sauce
1/4 cup red wine vinegar
1 teaspoon minced garlic
1/2 teaspoon ground ginger
1/4 teaspoon pepper

Cut steak into thin strips. Brown steak in hot oil until cooked through. In a saucepan, combine cornstarch and cold water. Whisk until smooth. Stir in sugar, soy sauce, vinegar, minced garlic, ginger and pepper. Heat to boiling. Cook and stir until thick and glossy. Pour sauce over steak and stir to coat. Allow to cool completely. Place steak and sauce in freezer bag or container. Label and freeze. 6 servings

To serve: Thaw and heat. Serve in bowls over rice.

 Freeze individual servings ready to heat and serve. Place cooked rice on bottom of individual serving-sized freezer containers. Top with chicken and sauce. Cover, label and freeze. **To serve:** Thaw and heat.

For **Teriyaki Chicken Bowls**, substitute 2 pounds boneless skinless chicken breast for the steak.

Sweet and Sour Chicken Bowls

2 pounds boneless skinless chicken breast
3 tablespoons canola oil
1/2 cup chunked onion
1/2 cup chunked green bell pepper
1 1/3 cups cold water
1/4 cup cornstarch
1/2 cup sugar
1/2 cup packed brown sugar
2/3 cup apple cider vinegar
1/4 cup soy sauce

Cut chicken into 1-inch cubes. Brown chicken in hot oil until cooked through. Add onion and green bell pepper. Cook and stir for about 1 minute. In a saucepan, combine water and cornstarch. Stir in sugar, brown sugar, soy sauce and vinegar. Heat to boiling. Cook and stir until thick and glossy. Pour sauce over chicken and stir to coat. Allow to cool completely. Place chicken and sauce in freezer bag or container. Label and freeze. 6 servings.

To serve: Thaw and heat. Serve in bowls over rice.

Freeze individual servings ready to heat and serve. Place cooked rice on bottom of individual serving-sized freezer containers. Top with chicken and sauce. Cover, label and freeze.

To serve: Thaw and heat.

Honey BBQ Wings

1 1/4 cups ketchup
1/3 cup apple cider vinegar
1/4 cup molasses
1/4 cup honey
1 teaspoon liquid smoke
1/2 teaspoon salt
1/4 teaspoon onion powder
1/4 teaspoon chili powder
12 chicken wings
1 egg, beaten
1 cup milk
2 cups flour
2 1/2 teaspoons salt
3/4 teaspoon pepper
oil for deep-frying

In a small saucepan, combine ketchup, vinegar, molasses, honey, liquid smoke, salt, onion powder and chili powder. Mix well. Bring to a boil over medium heat. Reduce heat. Simmer uncovered for about 20 minutes, until thickened. Separate chicken wings into 3 pieces. Discard wing tips. In a small bowl, combine egg and milk. In another small bowl, combine flour, salt and pepper. Dip each wing piece into flour mixture, then into egg mixture, then back into flour mixture. Arrange wings on a plate until all are coated. Fry wings in hot oil (350°) for 9 to12 minutes or until golden brown. Drain on paper towels. Brush wings with sauce. Arrange on foil-lined baking sheet. Place in freezer until completely frozen. Transfer wings to gallon freezer bag. Label and freeze. 24 pieces.

To serve: Thaw, heat and serve.

Chicken Nuggets

1 cup flour
4 teaspoons seasoned salt
1 teaspoon paprika
1 teaspoon ground mustard
1 teaspoon poultry seasoning
1/2 teaspoon pepper
2 pounds boneless skinless chicken breast
oil for cooking

In large bowl, combine flour, seasoned salt, paprika, ground mustard, poultry seasoning and pepper. Mix well. Pound chicken to 1/2-inch thickness. Cut into 1 1/2-inch pieces. A few at a time, place chicken pieces in bowl of seasoned flour. Stir to coat well. Heat about 1-inch of oil in skillet. Cook chicken, turning frequently until golden brown and cooked through. Allow to cool completely. Arrange in a single layer on baking sheet. Cover and place in freezer just until frozen. Transfer frozen nuggets to a gallon freezer bag. Label and freeze. 8 servings.

To serve: Heat in microwave. For crisper nuggets, thaw and broil or heat in toaster oven. Serve with **Sweet and Sour Sauce** (page 273).

Breaded Chicken Nuggets

1 egg
1/2 cup water
3/4 cup flour
1 teaspoon salt
1/4 teaspoon pepper
2 pounds boneless skinless chicken breast
oil for deep-frying

In a bowl, beat egg and water until frothy. Stir in flour, salt and pepper until smooth. Cut chicken into 1-inch chunks. Dip chicken into batter, draining off excess. Cook chicken in hot oil, a few pieces at a time for about 4 minutes or until golden brown. Drain on paper towels. Allow to cool completely. Arrange in a single layer on baking sheet. Cover and place in freezer just until frozen. Transfer frozen nuggets to a gallon freezer bag. Label and freeze. 8 servings.

To serve: Heat in microwave. For crisper nuggets, thaw and broil or heat in toaster oven. Serve with **Apricot Mustard Sauce** (page 275).

Cajun Chicken Nuggets

1/2 cup dry bread crumbs
1 1/2 teaspoons chili powder
1 teaspoon cumin
1/4 teaspoon cayenne pepper
1 (1.25-ounce) envelope onion soup mix
2 pounds boneless skinless chicken breast
oil for cooking

In a shallow bowl, combine bread crumbs, chili powder, cumin, cayenne pepper and onion soup mix. Cut chicken into 1-inch pieces. Roll chicken in bread crumb mixture, coating well. Heat 1/2-inch of oil in large skillet. Cook chicken in hot oil over medium heat, turning once, until cooked through. Drain on paper towels. Allow to cool completely. Arrange in a single layer on baking sheet. Cover and place in freezer just until frozen. Transfer frozen nuggets to a gallon freezer bag. Label and freeze. 8 servings.

To serve: Heat in microwave. For crisper nuggets, thaw and broil or heat in toaster oven. Serve with **Honey Mustard Dressing** (page 266).

Chicken Fajitas

1 tablespoon cornstarch
2 teaspoons chili powder
1 teaspoon salt
1 teaspoon paprika
1 teaspoon sugar
3/4 teaspoon chicken bouillon
1/2 teaspoon onion powder
1/4 teaspoon garlic powder
1/4 teaspoon cayenne pepper
1/4 teaspoon cumin
1 pound boneless skinless chicken breast
2 tablespoons canola oil
1 green bell pepper
1 onion
1/3 cup water

In a small bowl, combine cornstarch, chili powder, salt, paprika, sugar, chicken bouillon, onion powder, garlic powder, cayenne pepper and cumin. Mix well. Cut chicken into thin strips. In a skillet, brown chicken strips in hot oil over medium heat. Cut green bell pepper and onion into thin slices. Add to chicken. Sprinkle combined seasonings over chicken and vegetables. Stir in water. Cook and stir for about 5 minutes or until chicken is cooked through and vegetables are tender. Remove from heat and allow to cool completely. Place in freezer bag or container. For individual servings, spray a muffin tin with non-stick cooking spray. Fill muffin cups with filling. Cover and place pan in freezer just until frozen. Pop out and place in gallon freezer bag. Label and freeze. 8 servings.

To serve: Thaw and heat. Spoon warm filling into warm tortillas. Top with sour cream, shredded lettuce and cheese. Roll up and serve.

Lemon Spare-Rib Sandwiches

3 pounds boneless pork ribs
1 (12-ounce) can frozen lemonade concentrate
1 1/2 cups water
3 tablespoons chili sauce
1 tablespoon packed brown sugar
1 1/2 teaspoons apple cider vinegar
2 teaspoons cornstarch

Place ribs in large, heavy pan with a lid. Cover with water and bring to a boil. Reduce heat. Cover and simmer for 1 hour. Drain water. Combine lemonade concentrate, water, chili sauce, brown sugar and vinegar. Pour sauce over ribs. Cover and simmer for about 1 hour, until ribs are very tender. Remove ribs from sauce and allow to cool. Shred meat and return to sauce. Allow to cool completely. Place in freezer bag or container. For individual servings, spray a muffin tin with non-stick cooking spray. Fill muffin cups with meat and sauce. Cover and place pan in freezer just until frozen. Pop out and place in gallon freezer bag. Label and freeze. 8 servings.

To serve: Thaw and heat. Serve on warm rolls.

Pork Chile Verde

1 1/2 pounds pork roast
3 tablespoons flour
2 tablespoons canola oil
1 teaspoon minced garlic
1 cup chopped onion
2 (4-ounce) cans diced green chiles
2 cups water
1 (15-ounce) can stewed tomatoes
1 teaspoon salt
1/2 teaspoon pepper

Trim roast. Cut into 1-inch cubes. Coat pork with flour. In heavy skillet, brown pork in hot oil for about 10 minutes. Reduce heat and add garlic, onion, green chiles, water, undrained tomatoes, salt and pepper. Mix well. Cover pan and simmer for at least 45 minutes, stirring occasionally. Do not allow mixture to stick and burn on bottom. Remove from heat and allow to cool completely. Place in freezer bag or container. For individual servings, spray a muffin tin with non-stick cooking spray. Fill muffin cups with filling. Cover and place pan in freezer just until frozen. Pop out and place in gallon freezer bag. Label and freeze. 8 servings.

To serve: Thaw and heat. Serve with warm tortillas and sour cream.

Taco Bean Salad

1 pound lean ground beef
1/2 cup chopped onion
1 (15-ounce) can pork and beans
1 (1.25-ounce) envelope taco seasoning
1/2 cup water

Brown ground beef with onion. Stir in beans, seasoning mix and water. Bring to a boil. Cover. Reduce heat to low. Simmer for 15 minutes. Allow to cool completely. Place in freezer bag or container. For individual servings, spray a muffin tin with non-stick cooking spray. Spoon filling into muffin cups. Cover and place pan in freezer just until frozen. Pop out and place in gallon freezer bag. Label and freeze. 8 servings.

To serve: Thaw and heat. Place in shallow dishes. Cover with lettuce, tomato and cheese. Top with sour cream and salsa. Serve with nacho cheese tortilla chips.

Stacked Tacos

2 pounds lean ground beef
1 (15-ounce) can tomato sauce
1 (28-ounce) can diced tomatoes
2 cups salsa
1 (10.75-ounce) can tomato soup
1 (1.25-ounce) envelope taco seasoning

In large saucepan, brown ground beef, stirring often to break into small pieces. Add tomato sauce, diced tomatoes, salsa, tomato soup and taco seasoning. Simmer for about one hour. Place in freezer bag or container. For individual servings, spray a muffin tin with non-stick cooking spray. Spoon filling into muffin cups. Cover and place pan in freezer just until frozen. Pop out and place in gallon freezer bag. Label and freeze. 12 servings.

To serve: Thaw and heat filling. Heat oil in a skillet. For each serving, cook 3 corn tortillas in hot oil for about 15 seconds on each side. Drain on paper towels. Place one hot tortilla on plate. Spoon about 2 tablespoons meat mixture on tortilla. Sprinkle with shredded Cheddar cheese. Cover with another hot tortilla. Add about 1/4 cup meat mixture and sprinkle with cheese. Cover with 3rd hot tortilla, 1/4 cup meat mixture and cheese. Top with lettuce, olives and a heaping tablespoon of sour cream.

Chicken Spring Rolls

3 tablespoons peanut oil
6 cups shredded cabbage
2 cups bean sprouts
1/2 cup sliced onion
1 cup shredded carrots
1 1/2 cups cooked, shredded chicken
1/4 cup soy sauce
2 tablespoons sugar
1/2 teaspoon garlic salt
1 (16-ounce) package egg roll wraps
oil for deep-frying

Heat oil in large skillet. Add cabbage, bean sprouts, onion and carrots. Stir-fry until vegetables are nearly tender. Stir in chicken. Combine soy sauce, sugar and garlic salt. Add to skillet. Continue to cook and stir for about 1 minute. Divide cabbage mixture among egg roll wraps. With wrap in diamond shape, bring bottom corner up over cabbage filling. Moisten top edges with water. Fold both sides toward center. Roll up and seal. Cook rolls in hot oil, a few at a time, for about 5 minutes turning often, until golden brown. Allow to cool completely. Place in single layer in gallon freezer bags. Label and freeze. 15 servings.

To serve: Heat in microwave or for crisper egg roll, thaw and heat in broiler or toaster oven. Serve with soy sauce or **Sweet and Sour Sauce** (page 273).

Coney Island Dogs

1/2 pound lean ground beef
1/4 cup chopped onion
2 tablespoons minced celery
1/4 teaspoon salt
dash pepper
1 (8-ounce) can tomato sauce
2 tablespoons packed brown sugar
1 tablespoon Worcestershire sauce
1 tablespoon white vinegar
1 teaspoon chili powder
1 tablespoon ketchup
1/2 teaspoon mustard

Place ground beef, onion and celery in a skillet. Sprinkle with salt and pepper. Cook over medium heat until beef is browned, stirring often to break meat into very small pieces. Stir in tomato sauce, brown sugar, Worcestershire sauce, vinegar, chili powder, ketchup and mustard. Bring to a boil. Reduce heat and simmer uncovered for 20 minutes. Allow to cool completely. Place in freezer bag or container. For individual servings, spray a muffin tin with non-stick cooking spray. Fill muffin cups with chili. Cover and place pan in freezer just until frozen. Pop out and place in gallon freezer bag. Label and freeze. 8 servings.

To serve: Thaw and heat until bubbly. Spoon sauce over grilled hot dogs in buns.

Chili Dogs

3/4 pound lean ground beef
1/4 pound ground pork
6 cups water
1/4 cup cornstarch
1/4 cup flour
1/4 cup chili powder
1 (6-ounce) can tomato paste
3 tablespoons white vinegar
1 tablespoon salt
1 tablespoon minced dried onion
2 teaspoons sugar
1/4 teaspoon garlic powder
1/4 teaspoon pepper

Brown ground beef and ground pork, stirring often to break meat into very small pieces. Continue to simmer for about 10 minutes. In a large bowl, combine water, cornstarch and flour. Whisk until dissolved. Add to meat and stir well. Add chili powder, tomato paste, vinegar, salt, minced dried onion, sugar, garlic powder and pepper. Mix well. Bring to a boil over medium heat, stirring often. When chili boils, reduce heat and simmer for 30 minutes. Allow to cool completely. Place in freezer bag or container. For individual servings, spray a muffin tin with non-stick cooking spray. Fill muffin cups with chili. Cover and place pan in freezer just until frozen. Pop out and place in gallon freezer bag. Label and freeze. 12 servings.

To serve: Thaw and heat until bubbly. Spoon sauce over hot dogs in buns. Top with shredded cheese and chopped onions.

 This delicious chili is fabulous as **Chili Cheese Burgers** or **Chili Cheese Fries**.

Old Fashioned Chili

1 pound lean ground beef
1/2 cup chopped onion
1 (15-ounce) can tomato sauce
1 (15-ounce) can kidney beans
1 (15-ounce) can pinto beans
1 (4-ounce) can diced green chiles
2 tablespoons diced celery
1 cup chopped tomato
1 tablespoon packed brown sugar
1 teaspoon cumin
1 1/2 teaspoons chili powder
1/2 teaspoon pepper
1 teaspoon salt
1 cup water

In large saucepan, brown ground beef with onion. Add tomato sauce, undrained kidney beans and undrained pinto beans. Stir in green chiles, celery and tomato. Stir in brown sugar, cumin, chili powder, pepper, salt and water. Bring to a boil. Reduce heat. Simmer over low heat for 2 hours. Allow to cool. Place in freezer bag or in containers for single servings. Label and freeze. 6 servings.

To serve: Thaw and heat until bubbly. Serve with shredded Cheddar cheese and sour cream.

Chili is delicious served as **Taco Salad** (page 248). For easy individual **Taco Salad** servings, freeze **Old Fashioned Chili** in muffin tins.

Steak Chili Soup

1 pound beef round steak
2 tablespoons canola oil
2 (14.5-ounce) cans beef broth
1 (15-ounce) can small red beans
1 (14.5-ounce) can diced tomatoes
1 cup tomato vegetable juice
1/2 cup chopped green bell pepper
1/2 cup chopped red bell pepper
1 cup chopped onion
1 teaspoon minced garlic
1 teaspoon sugar
1 tablespoon chili powder
1/4 teaspoon cumin

Cut steak into small cubes. Brown beef in hot oil in large saucepan. Add broth. Bring to a boil. Reduce heat. Cover and simmer for 1 hour. Add undrained beans, undrained tomatoes, tomato vegetable juice, green bell pepper, red bell pepper, onion, garlic, sugar, chili powder and cumin. Cover and simmer for about 30 minutes. Allow to cool completely. Place in freezer bag or in containers for individual servings. Label and freeze. 6 servings.

To serve: Thaw and heat. Remove from heat and stir in cubed Monterey Jack cheese. Stir until cheese is partially melted. Ladle into bowls. Top with additional shredded cheese.

 For spicier **Steak Chili Soup**, substitute hot tomato vegetable juice for the tomato vegetable juice.

Beef Taco Soup

2 pounds lean ground beef
1 cup chopped onion
1 (28-ounce) can stewed tomatoes
2 cups tomato sauce
1 cup water
1 cup frozen corn
1 (15-ounce) can pinto beans
1 (1.25-ounce) envelope taco seasoning

Brown ground beef with onion. Add tomatoes, tomato sauce, water, corn, undrained beans and taco seasoning. Bring to a boil. Reduce heat and simmer for 20 minutes. Allow to cool completely. Place in freezer bag or in containers for individual servings. Label and freeze. 10 servings.

To serve: Thaw and heat. Top with sour cream, sliced avocado and chopped tomato. Serve with tortilla chips.

Pizza Soup

1/2 pound lean ground beef
1/2 pound Italian sausage
1/2 cup chopped onion
1/2 cup chopped green pepper
1 cup sliced mushrooms
1 teaspoon minced garlic
1 (2.25-ounce) can sliced black olives
1 (28-ounce) can stewed tomatoes
1 cup tomato sauce
1 cup beef broth
1 (4-ounce) package sliced pepperoni

Brown ground beef and Italian sausage with onion, green pepper, mushrooms and garlic. Add drained olives, stewed tomatoes, tomato sauce, beef broth and pepperoni. Bring to a boil. Reduce heat. Partially cover and simmer for 20 minutes. Allow to cool completely. Place in freezer bag or in containers for individual servings. Label and freeze. 10 servings.

To serve: Thaw and heat. Top with shredded Mozzarella cheese. Serve with garlic bread.

Steak Soup

1 1/2 pounds beef sirloin steak
1/2 cup butter
1 cup flour
6 1/2 cups water
1 (28-ounce) can diced tomatoes
1 (16-ounce) bag frozen mixed vegetables
1 cup chopped onion
1 cup chopped celery
1 (1.25-ounce) envelope brown gravy mix
2 teaspoons sugar
1/2 teaspoon pepper

Cut steak into thin strips. Brown sliced steak in butter. Stir in flour to form a smooth paste. Add water, stirring constantly. Bring to a boil. Cook and stir for 2 minutes or until thickened. Stir in tomatoes, mixed vegetables, onion, celery, gravy mix, sugar and pepper. Bring to a boil. Reduce heat. Cover and simmer 30 to 40 minutes. Allow to cool completely. Place in freezer bag or in containers for individual servings. Label and freeze. 10 servings.

To serve: Thaw and heat. Serve with Texas toast.

Steak and Vegetable Soup

1 1/2 pounds beef sirloin steak
2 tablespoons olive oil
1 teaspoon salt
1/2 teaspoon pepper
1 cup chopped onion
2 teaspoons minced garlic
1 cup sliced celery
1 cup sliced carrots
1 (10.75-ounce) can tomato soup
1 (1.25-ounce) envelope onion soup mix
1 (12-ounce) can tomato vegetable juice
1 (15-ounce) can creamed corn
4 cups water
2 cups frozen green beans
1 tablespoon sugar

Cut steak into thin strips. Brown steak in oil. Season with salt and pepper. Stir in onion, garlic, celery and carrots. Cook and stir until vegetables begin to soften. Stir in tomato soup, onion soup mix, tomato vegetable juice, creamed corn, water, green beans and sugar. Bring to a boil. Reduce heat and simmer for 45 minutes. Add additional salt and pepper to taste. Allow to cool completely. Place in freezer bag or in containers for individual servings. Label and freeze. 10 servings.

To serve: Thaw and heat. Serve with rolls and butter.

Beef Vegetable Soup

1 1/2 pounds lean ground beef
1/2 cup chopped onion
1 (46-ounce) can tomato vegetable juice
1 (16-ounce) bag frozen mixed vegetables
2 tablespoons beef bouillon
1 teaspoon sugar
1/2 teaspoon salt
1/4 teaspoon pepper

Brown ground beef with onion. Add tomato vegetable juice, frozen mixed vegetables, beef bouillon, sugar, salt and pepper. Bring to a boil. Reduce heat and simmer for 30 minutes. Allow to cool completely. Place in freezer bag or in containers for individual servings. Label and freeze. 8 servings.

To serve: Thaw and heat.

Beef and Bacon Soup

1/2 pound lean ground beef
1/2 pound diced bacon
1/2 cup chopped onion
2 (15-ounce) cans butter beans
1 (16-ounce) bag frozen mixed vegetables
1 cup cubed ham
1 (10.5-ounce) can tomato soup
1 cup tomato juice
2 teaspoons sugar
3/4 teaspoon salt
1/4 teaspoon pepper

Brown ground beef, bacon and onion. Stir in beans, frozen mixed vegetables, ham, tomato soup, tomato juice, sugar, salt and pepper. Bring to a boil. Reduce heat and simmer for 30 minutes. Add more tomato juice, if desired. Allow to cool completely. Place in freezer bag or in containers for individual servings. Label and freeze. 10 servings.

To serve: Thaw and heat. Serve with corn bread.

Beef Minestrone

1 pound beef sirloin steak
1/3 cup olive oil
3 tablespoons butter
1 cup chopped onion
1 1/2 cups sliced carrots
1 cup sliced celery
1 cup green beans
1 1/2 cups sliced zucchini
2 cups shredded cabbage
1 teaspoon minced garlic
2 (14.5-ounce) cans beef broth
1 (28-ounce) can diced tomatoes
1 teaspoon salt
1 teaspoon sugar
1/2 teaspoon basil
1/4 teaspoon pepper
1 bay leaf
1 (15-ounce) can cannellini beans

Cut steak into small pieces. In large pan, cook steak and onion in oil and butter until soft but not brown. Stir in carrots, celery and green beans. Cook and stir for 5 minutes. Stir in zucchini, cabbage and garlic. Cook and stir for 1 minute. Add broth, tomatoes, salt, sugar, basil, pepper, and bay leaf. Heat to boiling. Reduce heat. Simmer, covered, for about 1 1/2 hours. Stir in undrained beans. Cook, uncovered over medium heat, for 30 to 40 minutes, until soup is thick. Remove bay leaf. Allow to cool. Place in freezer bag or in containers for individual servings. Label and freeze. 10 servings.

To serve: Thaw and heat. Serve with garlic bread.

Italian Vegetable Soup

1 pound Italian sausage
1/2 cup chopped onion
1 teaspoon minced garlic
1 (15-ounce) can garbanzo beans
1 (14.5-ounce) can Italian tomatoes
1 1/2 cups sliced zucchini
1 (14.5-ounce) can beef broth
1 1/2 cups water
1/2 teaspoon basil
1/2 teaspoon salt
1 teaspoon sugar
1/4 teaspoon pepper

In large saucepan, brown Italian sausage with onion and garlic. Stir in undrained beans, tomatoes, zucchini, beef broth, water, basil, salt, sugar and pepper. Bring to a boil. Reduce heat and simmer for 20 minutes. Allow to cool completely. Place in freezer bag or in containers for individual servings. Label and freeze. 8 servings.

To serve: Thaw and heat. Top with shredded fresh Parmesan cheese. Serve with garlic toast.

Corn and Sausage Chowder

1 (8-ounce) package frozen breakfast sausage links
1 (14.5-ounce) can chicken broth
2 cups cubed potato
3/4 cup chopped onion
1/2 cup chopped celery
1 (11-ounce) can corn with red and green peppers
1 (15-ounce) can creamed corn
2 cups milk
1 teaspoon sugar
1 teaspoon salt
1/4 teaspoon pepper

Brown sausage and cut into 1/2-inch slices. In a large saucepan, combine chicken broth, potato, onion and celery. Simmer until potato is tender. Stir in sausage, corn, creamed corn, milk, sugar, salt and pepper. Partially cover and simmer for about 30 minutes. Allow to cool completely. Place in freezer bag or in containers for individual servings. Label and freeze. 8 servings.

To serve: Thaw. Heat and stir until smooth. Thin soup with a little milk, if necessary.

Bean and Cheese Soup

1 pound dry Navy beans
1 cup chopped onion
2 teaspoons minced garlic
1/2 cup diced carrots
1 cup chopped celery
1 cup diced ham
1/4 cup olive oil
3 quarts water
1 cups shredded fresh Parmesan cheese
1 teaspoon salt
1/4 teaspoon pepper

Place beans in a large pan. Cover with water and bring to a boil. Boil for two minutes. Remove from heat and let stand for 1 hour. Drain cooking water. Cook onion, garlic, carrots, celery and ham in olive oil for about 5 minutes. Add to beans. Add water. Bring to a boil. Reduce heat, partially cover and simmer for 1 1/2 hours. Remove half the beans and mash. Return to soup. Stir in cheese, salt and pepper. Allow to cool completely. Place in freezer bag or in containers for individual servings. Label and freeze. 8 servings.

To serve: Thaw and heat. Top with shredded fresh Parmesan cheese.

Chile Cheese Soup

1 cup chopped onion
1 cup chopped celery
1 cup shredded carrots
1/2 cup butter
1/2 cup flour
2 teaspoons ground mustard
2 teaspoons Worcestershire sauce
2 (14.5-ounce) cans chicken broth
3 cups milk
2 (4-ounce) cans diced green chiles
2 cups cooked, chopped chicken
1/2 teaspoon salt
1 (16-ounce) jar processed American cheese

In a large saucepan, cook onion, celery and carrots in butter until soft. Stir in flour, ground mustard, Worcestershire sauce and chicken broth. Heat and stir until smooth. Stir in milk, green chiles, chicken and salt. Bring to a boil. Reduce heat. Simmer for 30 minutes. Remove from heat. Stir in cheese and allow to melt. Allow to cool completely. Place in freezer bag or in containers for individual servings. Label and freeze. 6 servings.

To serve: Thaw. Heat and stir until smooth. Thin soup with broth if necessary. Serve with warm tortilla chips.

Garden Tomato Soup

1 pound boneless skinless chicken breast
2 tablespoons olive oil
1/4 cup butter
1 cup sliced celery
1/3 cup chopped onion
1/2 cup shredded carrots
1/3 cup chopped green bell pepper
4 cups chicken broth
4 cups peeled, chopped tomatoes
1 tablespoon sugar
1/2 teaspoon curry powder
1/2 teaspoon salt
1/4 teaspoon pepper
1/2 cup chicken broth
1/4 cup flour

Cut chicken into bite-sized pieces. In a large saucepan, brown chicken in oil. Add butter, celery, onion, carrots and green bell pepper. Cook until vegetables are soft but not brown. Add broth, tomatoes, sugar, curry, salt and pepper. Bring to a boil. Reduce heat. Simmer uncovered for 20 minutes. In a small bowl, combine chicken broth and flour until smooth. Stir into soup. Bring to a boil. Cook and stir until thickened and bubbly. Allow to cool completely. Place in freezer bag or in containers for individual servings. Label and freeze. 8 servings.

To serve: Thaw. Heat and stir until smooth. Serve with warm rolls and butter.

 Ripe garden fresh tomatoes make the very best **Garden Tomato Soup**. If garden fresh tomatoes are not available (sigh), substitute 1 (28-ounce) can diced tomatoes.

Chicken, Tomato and Mushroom Soup

2 cups sliced mushrooms
2 tablespoons butter
2 (14.5-ounce) cans chicken broth
2 cups cooked diced chicken
1 (14.5-ounce) can diced tomatoes
1 (8-ounce) can tomato sauce
1/2 cup sliced carrots
1 (.7-ounce) envelope Italian dressing mix
3/4 cup uncooked rice

Cook mushrooms in butter until soft and liquid has evaporated. Add broth, diced chicken, tomatoes, tomato sauce, carrots and dressing mix. Cover and simmer for 15 to 20 minutes, until carrots are tender. Remove from heat. Cook rice according to package directions. Stir in rice. Allow to cool completely. Place in freezer bag or in containers for individual servings. Label and freeze. 8 servings.

To serve: Thaw and heat.

Mexican Chicken Soup

1 pound boneless skinless chicken breast
4 cups water
1 cup chopped celery
1 cup chopped onion
2 cups sliced zucchini
1 cup sliced carrots
1 cup frozen corn
4 teaspoons minced garlic
1 (14.5-ounce) can Mexican tomatoes
1 (14.5-ounce) can diced tomatoes
1 (8-ounce) can tomato sauce
1 (4-ounce) can diced green chiles
1 cup **Chunky Salsa** (page 287)
1 tablespoon sugar
2 teaspoons chili powder
2 teaspoons cumin
1/2 teaspoon salt

Cut chicken into small pieces. Place chicken and water in a heavy pan with a lid. Add celery, onion, zucchini, carrots, corn and garlic. Stir in undrained Mexican tomatoes, undrained tomatoes, tomato sauce, green chiles, salsa, sugar, chili powder, cumin and salt. Mix well. Bring to a boil. Reduce heat. Cover and simmer for 40 minutes. Remove from heat. Allow to cool completely. Place in freezer bag or in containers for individual servings. Label and freeze. 6 servings.

To serve: Thaw and heat. Serve with nachos.

Southwest Chicken Vegetable Soup

1 1/2 pounds boneless skinless chicken thighs
6 cups chicken broth
1 (14.5-ounce) can diced tomatoes
1 cup water
1 (15-ounce) kidney beans
1 cup frozen corn
1 cup frozen green beans
1 (4-ounce) can diced green chiles
1/2 cup chopped onion
1/2 cup tomato sauce
6 corn tortillas
1 1/2 teaspoons chili powder
1/8 teaspoon garlic powder

Cut chicken into 1-inch cubes. In a large saucepan, combine chicken, broth, tomatoes and water. Stir in undrained beans, corn, green beans, green chiles, onion and tomato sauce. Cut tortillas into small pieces. Add to soup. Stir in chili powder and garlic powder. Bring to a boil. Reduce heat. Simmer for about 1 hour or until the tortilla pieces are mostly dissolved. Allow to cool completely. Place in freezer bag or in containers for individual servings. Label and freeze. 8 servings.

To serve: Thaw and heat. Top each bowl with shredded cheese and tortilla or corn chips.

Chile Corn Chowder

1/4 cup butter
1/2 cup chopped onion
2 tablespoon flour
2 cups chicken broth
2 cups diced potato
4 cups half-and-half
2 cups fresh corn
1 (4-ounce) can diced green chiles
2 cups cooked, chopped chicken
1 teaspoon garlic salt
1/4 teaspoon pepper

Melt butter in large saucepan. Cook onion in butter until soft but not brown. Stir in flour. Add chicken broth, stirring constantly until smooth. Add potato. Bring to a boil. Reduce heat. Cover and simmer for 10 to 15 minutes or until potato is tender. Add half-and-half, corn, green chiles, chicken, garlic salt and pepper. Cover and simmer for 15 minutes. Allow to cool completely. Place in freezer bag or in containers for individual servings. Label and freeze. 8 servings.

To serve: Thaw. Heat and stir until smooth. Thin soup with a little milk, if necessary.

Fresh sweet corn makes the very best **Chile Corn Chowder**. However, if fresh corn is unavailable (sigh), substitute frozen corn.

Chicken Bisque

2 quarts chicken broth
3 cups cooked, chopped chicken
1/4 cup sliced green onions
2 teaspoons chicken bouillon
1 teaspoon salt
1/2 teaspoon pepper
1 teaspoon sugar
1/2 cup butter
1 cup flour

In a large pan, combine chicken broth, chopped chicken, green onions, chicken bouillon, salt, pepper and sugar. Bring to a simmer. Melt butter in a small saucepan. Stir in flour to form a smooth paste. Cook and stir for 2 minutes. Stirring constantly, add flour paste to soup. Stir until smooth. Bring to a boil. Reduce heat. Simmer uncovered for 15 minutes. Allow to cool completely. Place in freezer bag or in containers for individual servings. Label and freeze. 8 servings.

To serve: Thaw. Heat and stir until smooth. Thin soup with a little broth, if necessary.

Chicken Corn Soup

2 pounds boneless skinless chicken breast
6 cups water
1 small onion
1 celery stalk
1 carrot
1 teaspoon salt
1 tablespoon chicken bouillon
1/2 cup chopped onion
1 cup shredded carrots
1 cup very thin sliced celery
1 tablespoon dried parsley flakes
1 tablespoon sugar
2 cups fresh corn
1 quart half-and-half
1/8 teaspoon pepper

Place chicken and water in a large pan. Cut onion, celery and carrot in half. Add to pan with chicken. Add salt. Bring to a boil. Reduce heat and cook for about 30 minutes, until chicken is tender. Remove chicken and cut into chunks. Remove vegetables and discard. Return chicken to pan. Add chicken bouillon, chopped onion, shredded carrots, sliced celery, parsley flakes, sugar and corn. Cook for about 30 minutes. Add more water if necessary. Remove from heat. Stir in half-and-half and pepper. Add salt to taste. Allow to cool completely. Place in freezer bag or in containers for individual servings. Label and freeze. 10 servings.

To serve: Thaw. Heat and stir until smooth. Thin soup with a little milk, if necessary.

 Fresh corn makes the best **Chicken Corn Soup**. However, if fresh corn is not available (it is seasonal, after all) substitute frozen corn.

Chicken and Rice Soup

1 pound boneless skinless chicken breast
10 cups chicken broth
1 cup chopped onion
1 cup sliced celery
1 cup sliced carrots
1 teaspoon salt
1 teaspoon sugar
1/2 teaspoon pepper
1 bay leaf
1 cup uncooked rice

Cut chicken into 1-inch cubes. In a large pan, combine chicken, chicken broth, onion, celery, carrots, salt, sugar, pepper and bay leaf. Bring to a boil. Reduce heat and simmer uncovered for 30 minutes. Remove from heat. Remove bay leaf. Cook rice according to package directions. Stir in rice. Allow to cool completely. Place in freezer bag or in containers for individual servings. Label and freeze. 10 servings.

To serve: Thaw and heat.

Turkey and Wild Rice Soup

1 cup wild rice
1/2 cup butter
1/2 cup chopped onion
1/2 cup sliced celery
1 cup sliced carrots
1/2 cup flour
2 (14.5-ounce) cans chicken broth
2 cups cooked, chopped turkey
2 cups cream
1 teaspoon salt
1/4 teaspoon pepper
2 teaspoons sugar

Cook rice according to package directions. Melt butter in a large pan. Cook onion, celery and carrots in butter until soft. Stir in flour. Cook and stir for 2 minutes. Stir in chicken broth. Bring to a boil. Cook for 1 minute. Stir in cooked wild rice, chopped turkey, cream, salt, pepper and sugar. Bring to a boil. Reduce heat and simmer for 20 minutes. Allow to cool completely. Place in freezer bag or in containers for individual servings. Label and freeze. 8 servings.

To serve: Thaw. Heat and stir until smooth. Thin soup with a little milk, if necessary.

Turkey Chowder

2 cups cooked, diced turkey
2 (15-ounce) cans creamed corn
2 1/2 cups milk
1 cup chicken broth
1 cup diced potato
1/2 cup shredded carrots
1/2 cup chopped onion
1 teaspoon salt
1/4 teaspoon pepper

In a large pan, combine turkey, corn, milk and broth. Stir in potato, carrots, onion, salt and pepper. Bring to a boil. Reduce heat. Cover and simmer for 25 minutes. Allow to cool completely. Place in freezer bag or in containers for individual servings. Label and freeze. 8 servings.

To serve: Thaw. Heat and stir until smooth. Thin soup with a little milk, if necessary.

Broccoli Cheese Soup

3 cups water
2 tablespoons chicken bouillon
2 (10-ounce) packages frozen chopped broccoli
4 cups half-and-half
1 teaspoon salt
1/4 teaspoon pepper
1 teaspoon sugar
1/2 cup flour
1 cup water
1 1/2 cups shredded Swiss cheese
1 cup shredded Cheddar cheese

In large saucepan, combine 3 cups water and chicken bouillon. Heat until bouillon is dissolved. Add broccoli. Cover and cook until tender, about 8 minutes. Stir in half-and-half, salt, pepper and sugar. Combine flour and water. Stir into soup. Cook and stir over medium heat for about 3 minutes or until thick and bubbly. Remove from heat. Add Swiss and Cheddar cheese. Stir until partially melted. Allow to cool completely. Place in freezer bag or in containers for individual servings. Label and freeze. 10 servings.

To serve: Thaw. Heat and stir until smooth. Thin soup with a little milk, if necessary. Top with shredded cheese.

Broccoli and Cheddar Chowder

1/2 cup butter
1/3 cup flour
1 (14.5-ounce) can chicken broth
1 (10.75-ounce) can Cheddar cheese soup
2 cups milk
2 cups cream
1 (16-ounce) package frozen chopped broccoli
1 teaspoon sugar
1 teaspoon salt
1/2 teaspoon pepper

Melt butter in a large pan. Stir in flour. Cook and stir until bubbly. Stir in chicken broth. Cook and stir until mixture begins to thicken. Add soup, milk and cream. Stir until smooth. Add broccoli, sugar, salt and pepper. Cook over medium heat for about 8 minutes, until broccoli is tender. Allow to cool completely. Place in freezer bag or in containers for individual servings. Label and freeze. 8 servings.

To serve: Thaw. Heat and stir until smooth. Thin soup with a little milk, if necessary.

Butternut Soup

3 pounds butternut squash
6 cups chicken broth
1 1/2 cups sliced zucchini
3 leeks
2 cups chopped carrots
1/3 cup butter
2 teaspoons salt
1/4 teaspoon pepper
1 cup half-and-half
1/2 cup milk

Peel and cube the butternut squash. Place in a large pan with chicken broth and zucchini. Slice the white section of the leeks. In a separate pan, cook sliced leeks and carrots in butter until tender. Place in pan with squash, chicken broth and zucchini. Add salt and pepper. Cook over medium heat until squash is very soft, about 40 minutes. Using electric mixer, mix until soup is mostly smooth. Remove from heat and add half-and-half and milk. Allow to cool completely. Place in freezer bag or in containers for individual servings. Label and freeze. 10 servings.

To serve: Thaw. Heat and stir until smooth. Thin soup with a little milk, if necessary. Top with shredded fresh Parmesan cheese.

To peel and cube a butternut squash, lay squash on its side on a cutting board. Using a large, sharp knife, cut squash in 3/4-inch thick slices. Using a paring knife, peel each slice. Lay peeled slices on cutting board and, using a large sharp knife, cut each slice into 3/4-inch thick strips. Then cut the strips into 3/4-inch cubes.

Peanut Butter Soup

1/2 pound lean ground beef
1 tablespoon canola oil
1/2 cup finely chopped onion
1/2 cup finely chopped celery
1 cup diced carrots
2 cups cubed potato
1 cup smooth peanut butter
2 teaspoons beef bouillon
1 (16-ounce) can tomato paste
1/2 cup peanuts
4 cups water
1/2 teaspoon salt
1/8 teaspoon pepper

Brown ground beef in a large saucepan. Add oil, onion, celery and carrots. Cook and stir until vegetables are tender and beginning to brown. Stir in potato, peanut butter, bouillon, tomato paste, peanuts, water, salt and pepper. Bring to a boil. Reduce heat to medium-low and simmer for 30 minutes. Allow to cool completely. Place in freezer bag or in containers for individual servings. Label and freeze. 6 servings.

To serve: Thaw and heat.

 Substitute 1 1/2 cups crunchy peanut butter for the smooth peanut butter and peanuts, if desired.

Oven Assemble Recipes

Pork Skewers

1/2 cup pineapple juice
3 tablespoons Worcestershire sauce
1 teaspoon minced garlic
1/4 teaspoon crushed red pepper flakes
1/8 teaspoon pepper
1 pound boneless pork loin
8 bamboo skewers

In a small bowl, combine pineapple juice, Worcestershire sauce, garlic, red pepper flakes and pepper. Cut pork into very thin slices. Place pork in sauce. Refrigerate and allow to marinate for about 1 hour. Weave pork strips onto skewers so that the meat lies flat. Broil, 4 inches from heat for about 2 minutes on each side or until cooked through. Allow to cool. Place in freezer bag, being careful to not pierce bag with skewers. Label and freeze. 8 skewers.

To serve: Thaw and heat.

Teriyaki Beef Strips

1/4 cup soy sauce
1 cup water
1/2 cup packed brown sugar
2 tablespoons cornstarch
2 tablespoons sesame oil
1/4 cup chopped green onion
1 teaspoon minced garlic
1 teaspoon minced ginger
2 1/2 pounds beef sirloin steak
16 bamboo skewers

In a small saucepan, combine soy sauce, water, brown sugar and cornstarch. Whisk until sugar is dissolved and mixture is smooth. Stir in oil, green onion, garlic and ginger. Simmer, stirring constantly until thickened. Remove from heat and set aside. Cut steak into very thin strips about 1-inch wide and 4-inches long. Thread beef onto skewers, keeping meat as flat as possible. Brush both sides of beef with sauce. Place skewers on rack of broiler pan. Broil 4 inches from heat for about 2 minutes on each side or until cooked through. Allow to cool. Place in freezer bag, being careful to not pierce bag with skewers. Label and freeze. 16 skewers.

To serve: Thaw and heat.

Be sure to use sirloin steak or other very tender cuts of beef. Less tender cuts of beef may taste good but will probably turn out tough.

Teriyaki Beef Salad

1 recipe **Teriyaki Beef Strips** (page 190)
1/3 (6.75-ounce) package rice sticks
6 cups torn curly leaf lettuce
6 cups torn red curly leaf lettuce
1 red onion
1 (20-ounce) can pineapple rings
1/4 cup sliced green onion
Sweet Onion Sauce (page 278)

Prepare **Teriyaki Beef Strips** as directed. Allow to cool completely. Place skewers carefully in freezer bag. Label and freeze. 6 servings.

To serve: Place rice sticks in hot oil for a few seconds until they puff up. Pile rice sticks on a serving platter (or individual plates). Top with mixed lettuce. Slice red onion and separate rings. Arrange onion and drained pineapple rings over top of lettuce. Heat **Teriyaki Beef Strips** and place on top. Sprinkle with sliced green onion. Serve with **Sweet Onion Sauce**. 6 servings.

For an alternate presentation, omit skewers when preparing **Teriyaki Beef Strips**. Pile hot **Teriyaki Beef** on salad.

Rice sticks are usually found in the Oriental section of the grocery store. Another name for them is *Maifun*. Substitute beans threads or *Saifun,* if desired.

Buffalo Chicken Strips

1 (14-ounce) bottle hot-style ketchup
1/4 cup honey
2 tablespoons fresh lemon juice
1/2 teaspoon lemon pepper
1 1/2 pounds boneless skinless chicken breast
12 bamboo skewers

In a small bowl, combine hot ketchup, honey, lemon juice and lemon pepper. Whisk until smooth. Cut chicken lengthwise into long 1/2-inch thick strips. Thread chicken strips onto skewers, keeping strips as flat as possible. Coat chicken with sauce. Place in a single layer on a baking sheet. Broil 4 inches from heat for about 2 minutes on each side or until cooked through. Allow to cool. Place in freezer bag, being careful to not pierce bag with skewers. Label and freeze. 12 servings.

To serve: Thaw and heat. Serve with **Bleu Cheese Dressing** (page 270).

 For fresh lemon juice, place a lemon in a glass dish. Heat in the microwave until lemon bursts (about 1 minute). Immediately stop microwave. Allow to cool enough to handle. Lemon juice can then be easily squeezed from the hole made by the escaping steam.

For hotter **Buffalo Chicken Strips** add 1 to 3 teaspoons of hot pepper sauce.

Buffalo Chicken Salad

1 recipe **Buffalo Chicken Strips** (page 192)
12 cups torn red curly leaf lettuce
1 cup sliced celery
1/2 cup crumbled bleu cheese
Bleu Cheese Dressing (page 270)

Prepare **Buffalo Chicken Strips** as directed. Allow to cool completely. Place skewers carefully in freezer bag. Label and freeze. 6 servings.

To serve: Arrange lettuce and celery on a serving platter (or individual plates). Heat **Buffalo Chicken Strips** and pile on lettuce. Crumble bleu cheese over all. Serve with **Bleu Cheese Dressing**.

For an alternate presentation, omit skewers when preparing **Buffalo Chicken Strips**. Pile hot Buffalo Chicken on salad.

Beefy Corn Bread

1/2 pound lean ground beef
1 teaspoon chili powder
1/4 teaspoon cumin
1/2 cup frozen corn
1/4 cup salsa
1 cup shredded Cheddar cheese
3/4 cup corn meal
3/4 cup flour
2 tablespoons sugar
2 teaspoons baking powder
1/2 teaspoon salt
2 eggs
3/4 cup milk
2 tablespoons canola oil

Brown ground beef with chili powder and cumin until meat is no longer pink. Stir in corn and salsa. Line the cups of a muffin tin with foil baking cups. Spoon meat into muffin cups, filling cups 2/3 full. Top with cheese. In medium bowl, combine corn meal, flour, sugar, baking powder and salt. Beat eggs In a small bowl. Add milk and oil. Add to the cornmeal mixture, stirring just until moistened. Spoon batter over cheese to cover. Bake at 375° for 15 minutes. Allow to cool. Set pan in freezer until frozen. Remove from pan and place in gallon freezer bag. Label and freeze. 8 servings.

To serve: Thaw and heat in oven or toaster oven. To heat in the microwave, thaw upside down on microwave safe plate. Remove foil. Microwave until heated through.

 Foil baking cups can be found in the baking section, usually next to the paper muffin liners.

Beanie-Wienie Corn Bread

1 tablespoon canola oil
1/3 cup chopped green bell pepper
1/3 cup chopped onion
6 hot dogs
2 (15-ounce) cans pork and beans
1/4 cup barbeque sauce
2 tablespoons ketchup
1 tablespoon packed brown sugar
1 1/4 cups corn meal
1/4 cup flour
1 tablespoon baking powder
1 tablespoon sugar
1/4 teaspoon salt
3 tablespoons canola oil
1 cup milk
1 egg

In a large skillet, cook onion and bell pepper in oil until soft. Slice hot dogs. Add beans, sliced hot dogs, barbeque sauce, ketchup and brown sugar to skillet. Cook until heated through. Line the cups of a muffin tin with foil baking cups. Spoon filling into muffin cups, filling cups 2/3 full. In mixing bowl, combine corn meal, flour, baking powder, sugar and salt. Mix well. Add oil, milk and egg. Mix just until moistened. Spoon batter over bean mixture to cover. Bake uncovered at 350° for 15 minutes. Allow to cool completely. Set pan in freezer until frozen. Remove from pan and place in gallon freezer bag. Label and freeze. 18 servings.

To serve: Thaw and heat in oven or toaster oven. To heat in the microwave, thaw upside down on microwave safe plate. Remove foil. Microwave until heated through.

Pizza Biscuit Cups

1 pound lean ground beef
1 (14-ounce) jar spaghetti sauce
2 (16-ounce) cans large refrigerated biscuit dough
1 1/2 cups shredded Mozzarella cheese

In a skillet, brown ground beef. Stir in spaghetti sauce. Remove from heat. Press biscuits onto the bottom and up the sides of greased muffin cups. Spoon 2 table-spoonfuls meat mixture into center of each cup. Bake at 375° for 15 minutes or until golden brown. Sprinkle with cheese. Allow to cool completely. Set pan in freezer until frozen. Remove from pan and place in gallon freezer bag. Label and freeze. 16 servings.

To serve: Thaw and heat in microwave or in toaster oven.

Stuffed Pizza Rounds

1 (7.5-ounce) can layered refrigerated biscuit dough
1/4 cup spaghetti sauce
1/4 cup chopped pepperoni
1 tablespoon sliced black olives
3 tablespoons shredded Mozzarella cheese
2 tablespoons melted butter
1/4 teaspoon oregano
1/8 teaspoon garlic powder

Separate dough into 10 biscuits. Separate each biscuit into 2 layers. Place 10 layers on an ungreased baking sheet. Roll each to make a 2 1/2-inch round. Spoon about 1 heaping teaspoon of sauce onto each biscuit. Top with about 1 teaspoon chopped pepperoni. Sprinkle with black olive slices and cheese, keeping edges clean. Roll remaining biscuit layers into 2 1/2 inch rounds. Place over filling. Stretch to fit. Press edges with a fork to seal. Brush melted butter over tops. Sprinkle with oregano and garlic powder. Bake at 400° for 12 to 15 minutes or until golden brown. Allow to cool completely. Place in single layer in gallon freezer bag. Label and freeze. 10 rounds.

To serve: Thaw and heat in microwave. For a crisper crust, heat in toaster oven.

Mozzarella Puffs

1 (7.5-ounce) can refrigerated biscuit dough
10 (3/4-inch) cubes Mozzarella cheese
1 cup prepared spaghetti sauce

Separate dough into 10 biscuits. Place one cheese cube on center of each biscuit. Spoon about 1 teaspoon sauce onto each biscuit, keeping edges clean. Pinch dough tightly together to seal in cheese and sauce. Place seam side down on baking sheet. Spread sauce over top. Bake at 375° for 10 to 12 minutes. Allow to cool. Place baking sheet in freezer until puffs are frozen. Remove from pan and place in freezer bag. Label and freeze. 10 puffs.

To serve: Thaw. Heat briefly in microwave. Serve with additional warmed sauce, if desired.

For **Pepperoni Mozzarella Puffs**, place one pepperoni slice onto each biscuit before adding cheese and sauce.

Mini Taco Pies

1 1/2 pounds lean ground beef
1/2 cup chopped onion
1 (4-ounce) can diced green chiles
1 (1.25-ounce) envelope taco seasoning
1/2 cup water
2 cups shredded Cheddar cheese
1 cup milk
1 cup biscuit/baking mix
2 eggs

Brown ground beef with onion. Stir in green chiles, taco seasoning and water. Simmer uncovered for 5 minutes. Line the cups of a muffin tin with foil baking cups. Spoon meat into muffin cups. Sprinkle cheese over meat. In a bowl, combine milk, biscuit/baking mix and eggs. Mix until smooth. Spoon batter over cheese. Bake at 350° for 15 minutes. Allow to cool completely. Place in a single layer in gallon freezer bag. Label and freeze. 12 servings.

To serve: Thaw and heat in oven or toaster oven. To heat in the microwave, thaw upside down on microwave safe plate. Remove foil. Microwave until heated through.

 Foil baking cups can be found in the baking section, usually next to the paper muffin liners.

Pizza Roll-Ups

1 (16-ounce) loaf frozen bread dough
1 pound lean ground beef
1/4 cup chopped onion
1 teaspoon salt
1/2 teaspoon pepper
1 teaspoon Italian seasoning
2 cups shredded Mozzarella cheese

Thaw bread dough. Roll into a 14 x 24-inch rectangle, about 1/4-inch thick. Brown ground beef with onion, salt and pepper. Add Italian seasoning. Spread browned beef onto dough. Press in slightly. Top with cheese. Press slightly again. Roll up, starting on long side. Cut into 24 slices. Lay on greased baking sheets. Allow to rest and rise slightly for about 20 to 30 minutes. Bake at 350° for 20 to 25 minutes, or until golden brown. Allow to cool completely. Place in gallon freezer bag. Label and freeze. 24 servings.

To serve: Thaw. Heat in oven (about 10 minutes) or briefly in microwave. Serve with warm spaghetti sauce.

For quick individual servings, spoon spaghetti sauce into ice cube trays. Freeze until solid. Pop out and place spaghetti sauce "cubes" into a freezer bag. Use one "cube" for each Pizza Roll-Up.

Taco Crescents

3/4 pound lean ground beef
1/3 cup chopped onion
1 (1.25-ounce) envelope taco seasoning
1/4 cup water
2 eggs
1/2 cup Cheddar cheese
1/2 cup Monterey Jack cheese
2 (8-ounce) cans refrigerated crescent roll dough

Brown ground beef with onion. Add taco seasoning and water. Cook and stir until thoroughly mixed and most of the water is gone. Stir in eggs and cheese. Remove from heat. Unroll crescent roll dough. Separate into triangles. Place 2 tablespoons of taco mixture on the short side of each triangle. Starting with short side of triangle, roll up ending with point. Place on baking sheet. Bake at 375° for 10 to 15 minutes. Allow to cool. Place each **Taco Crescent** into a sandwich bag. Place individually wrapped crescents into a freezer bag. Label and freeze. 16 servings.

To serve: Thaw. Heat briefly in microwave. For crisper crescents, heat in toaster oven.

Cheeseburger Bites

1/2 pound lean ground beef
2 tablespoons minced onion
1/2 teaspoon Worcestershire sauce
1 egg yolk
1/2 teaspoon salt
pepper
6 slices bread
24 cubes Cheddar cheese

Combine ground beef, minced onion, Worcestershire sauce, egg yolk, salt and pepper. Mix well. Shape into 24 meatballs. Remove crust from bread. Roll flat and cut each flattened bread slice into four 1 1/2-inch rounds. On each round, place one meatball. Place one cheese cube into center of meatball. Press down to sink the cheese into the meatball and to partially flatten the meatball. Broil 3 to 5 minutes. Freeze in single layer in on baking sheet. Transfer to freezer bag. Label and freeze. 24 bites.

To serve: Thaw and heat briefly in microwave or in toaster oven.

Taco Tarts

1 pound lean ground beef
1/4 cup chopped onion
1 (1.25-ounce) envelope taco seasoning
2 tablespoons water
1 cup sour cream
2 tablespoons salsa
1 cup coarsely crushed tortilla chips
1 1/2 cups shredded Cheddar cheese

Combine ground beef, onion, taco seasoning and water. Mix well. Press onto bottom and up the sides of mini-muffin cups. Combine sour cream, salsa and crushed tortilla chips. Mix well. Place about 1 teaspoon filling into each meat shell. Top with shredded cheese. Press down lightly. Bake at 425° for 7 to 8 minutes. Allow to cool completely. Place pan into freezer until tarts are frozen. Pop out and place in freezer bag. Label and freeze. 10 servings.

To serve: Thaw and heat. Serve with salsa.

Taco Cups

2 (8-ounce) cans refrigerated biscuit dough
1 cup shredded Cheddar cheese
1 pound lean ground beef
1 (1.25-ounce) envelope taco seasoning
3/4 cup water
1/4 cup salsa
1 cup shredded Cheddar cheese

Separate biscuits. Press biscuits into the ungreased cups of muffin tins. Press cheese into the bottom of each cup. Brown ground beef. Stir in taco seasoning and water. Mix well. Simmer for about 5 minutes. Stir in salsa. Fill cups with taco filling. Bake, uncovered, at 350° for 12 minutes or until biscuit cups are browned. Remove from oven. Sprinkle each **Taco Cup** with cheese. Allow to cool completely. Remove from pan. Place in gallon freezer bag. Label and freeze. 20 servings.

To serve: Heat in microwave or thaw and heat in toaster oven. Top with sour cream and serve with salsa.

Chinese Triangles

1/2 pound lean ground beef
1 cup bean sprouts
1/2 cup sliced water chestnuts, finely chopped
2 tablespoons minced onion
1 envelope beef and mushroom dry soup mix
2 (8-ounce) cans refrigerated crescent roll dough

In a skillet, combine ground beef with bean sprouts, water chestnuts, onion and dry soup mix. Cook until beef is browned and onion is tender. Separate dough into triangles. Place about 1 tablespoon filling on each triangle. Fold dough over filling and pinch corners together to seal edges. Place on an ungreased baking sheet. Bake, uncovered at 375° for 15 minutes or until golden brown. Allow to cool. Place baking sheet in freezer until triangles are frozen. Transfer triangles to freezer bag. Label and freeze. 16 triangles.

To serve: Heat in microwave. For crisper crust, broil or heat in toaster oven. Serve with **Sweet and Sour sauce** (page 273).

Oven Chicken Nuggets

2 pounds boneless skinless chicken breast
1 cup cornflake crumbs
1 teaspoon garlic salt
1/4 teaspoon pepper
1/2 cup canned Parmesan cheese
Ranch Dressing (page 263)

Cut chicken into 1-inch cubes. In a shallow bowl, combine crumbs, garlic salt, pepper and Parmesan cheese. Place Ranch dressing in a separate bowl. Toss chicken cubes in dressing then roll in cornflake mixture. Place on a greased foil-lined baking sheet. Bake uncovered at 400° for 12 to 15 minutes. Allow to cool completely. Cover and freeze in a single layer on baking sheet. When frozen, transfer to a gallon freezer bag. Label and freeze. 8 servings.

To serve: Thaw and heat. Serve with **Ranch Dressing**.

Italian Cheese Chicken Nuggets

2 pounds boneless skinless chicken breast
3 tablespoons melted butter
2 teaspoons Worcestershire sauce
1/2 cup Italian bread crumbs
1/3 cup canned Parmesan cheese

Cut chicken into 1-inch pieces. Combine chicken, melted butter and Worcestershire sauce. In a shallow dish, combine crumbs and cheese. Roll chicken in crumbs. Arrange on baking sheet. Bake at 450° for 8 to 10 minutes. Cover and freeze in single layer on baking sheet. When frozen, transfer to a freezer bag. Label and freeze. 8 servings.

To serve: Heat in microwave. Serve with warm spaghetti sauce.

Sesame Chicken Nuggets

1/2 cup dry bread crumbs
1/4 cup sesame seeds
1/2 cup mayonnaise
1 teaspoon ground mustard
1 teaspoon minced dried onion
2 pounds boneless skinless chicken breast

In bowl, combine dry bread crumbs and sesame seeds. In separate bowl, combine mayonnaise, ground mustard and dried onion. Pound chicken to flatten to equal thickness and cut into 1-inch pieces. Coat chicken with mayonnaise mixture then roll in bread crumb mixture. Place on greased foil-lined baking sheet. Bake uncovered at 425° for 10 minutes or until golden brown and cooked through. Allow to cool completely. Arrange in a single layer on baking sheet. Cover and place in freezer just until frozen. Transfer frozen nuggets to a gallon freezer bag. Label and freeze. 8 servings.

To serve: Heat in microwave. For crisper nuggets, thaw and broil or heat in toaster oven. Serve with **Honey Mayonnaise** (page 284).

Sesame Chicken Salad

1 recipe **Sesame Chicken Nuggets** (page 208)
12 cups salad greens
1 cup julienned carrots
1 cup julienned celery
Ranch Dressing (page 263)

Prepare **Sesame Chicken Nuggets** as directed. Allow to cool completely. Place in freezer bag. Label and freeze. 6 servings.

To serve: Arrange salad greens on a serving platter (or individual plates). Arrange carrots and celery in two piles on lettuce. Heat **Sesame Chicken Nuggets** and arrange in a third pile on lettuce. Serve with **Ranch Dressing.**

Substitute **Oven Chicken Nuggets** (page 206), **Italian Cheese Chicken Nuggets** (page 207), **Chicken Nuggets** (page 150), **Breaded Chicken Nuggets** (page 151 or **Cajun chicken Nuggets** (page 152) for the **Sesame Chicken Nuggets.**

Sesame Chicken Skewers

4 boneless skinless chicken breast halves
1/2 cup hoisin sauce
1/2 cup orange marmalade
2 tablespoons honey
1/4 teaspoon cayenne pepper
1 teaspoon minced ginger
1 teaspoon minced garlic
16 (8-10 inch) bamboo skewers

Cut each breast half lengthwise into 4 strips. Thread one chicken strip onto each skewer. Place skewers on a foil-lined 15 x 10 x 1-inch baking pan. In small bowl, combine hoisin sauce, marmalade, honey, cayenne pepper, ginger and garlic. Mix well. Remove 1/2 cup sauce. Brush chicken with the 1/2 cup sauce. Reserve remaining sauce. Bake at 425° for 12 to 15 minutes, brushing chicken occasionally with pan drippings. Allow to cool. Place in freezer bag, being careful to not pierce bag with skewers. Label and freeze. Place reserved sauce in small freezer bag or container. Label and freeze. 16 skewers.

To serve: Thaw and heat. Serve chicken with sauce.

Hoisin sauce is found in the Oriental section of most grocery stores.

Coconut Chicken Fingers

1 cup chopped pecans
1 cup corn flake crumbs
1/2 cup sweetened flaked coconut
2 eggs, beaten
1 tablespoon milk
1/2 cup flour
1/4 teaspoon salt
8 chicken tenders, cut in half lengthwise
3 tablespoons melted butter

Process pecans in food processor until finely chopped. Add corn flake crumbs and coconut. Pulse to blend. Place in a shallow dish. In a separate dish, whisk together eggs and milk. In yet another dish, combine flour and salt. Dip chicken strips in flour mixture until completely coated. Dip flour coated chicken into egg mixture, then into pecan crumb mixture. Press coating onto chicken. Place coated chicken on a foil-lined, buttered baking sheet. Drizzle with melted butter. Bake at 400° for 10 to 15 minutes, until golden brown and cooked through. Allow to cool completely. Place cooked chicken strips into freezer and allow to freeze. When completely frozen, transfer strips to freezer bag. Label and return to freezer. 8 servings.

To serve: Thaw. Heat in microwave or in toaster oven. Serve with **Marmalade Dipping Sauce** (page 277).

Texas Tenders

1 pound chicken tenders
3 cups crisp rice cereal, crushed
1 teaspoon garlic salt
1 teaspoon chili powder
1/4 cup canola oil

Combine crushed rice cereal, garlic salt and chili powder. Dip chicken tenders first in oil, then roll in cereal mixture. Place on foil-lined baking sheet. Bake uncovered at 375° for 25 minutes. Allow to cool completely. Cover and place in freezer just until frozen. Transfer frozen tenders to a gallon freezer bag. Label and freeze. 6 servings.

To serve: Heat in microwave. For crisper tenders, thaw and broil or heat in toaster oven. Serve with **Green Chile Sour Cream** (page 281).

Chicken Squares

1 (3-ounce) package cream cheese
3 tablespoons melted butter
2 cups cooked, chopped chicken
1 tablespoon minced onion
1/4 teaspoon salt
1/8 teaspoon pepper
2 tablespoons milk
1 (8-ounce) can refrigerated crescent roll dough
2 tablespoons melted butter
3/4 cup crushed seasoned croutons

Combine cream cheese and melted butter. Add chicken, onion, salt, pepper and milk. Separate dough into 4 rectangles, pressing together perforations. Spoon 1/2 cup filling onto each rectangle. Fold dough over filling and press edges to seal. Brush tops with melted butter and sprinkle with crumbs. Bake at 350° for 20 to 25 minutes. Allow to cool. Place each in sandwich bag. Place individually wrapped squares into freezer bag. Label and freeze. 4 servings.

To serve: Thaw. Heat briefly in microwave. For crisper crust, heat in toaster oven.

To freeze unbaked **Chicken Squares**, combine filling ingredients and place in a freezer bag. Label and freeze. To serve: Thaw filling. Assemble and bake as directed above.

Chicken and Broccoli Calzones

2 cups cooked, shredded chicken
3/4 teaspoon salt
1/4 teaspoon crushed red pepper flakes
1 (10-ounce) package frozen chopped broccoli, thawed
1 cup Ricotta cheese
1 cup shredded Mozzarella cheese
1/3 cup shredded fresh Parmesan cheese
1 (16-ounce) loaf frozen bread dough, thawed

In bowl, combine shredded chicken, salt, red pepper flakes, broccoli and Ricotta cheese. Mix well. Stir in shredded Mozzarella and Parmesan cheese. Divide bread dough into 4 balls. On a lightly floured surface, roll each ball into a 9-inch circle. Place one fourth of the filling onto each, leaving a 1-inch border all around. Fold dough in half to enclose filling in a half moon shape. Press edges together with a fork to seal. Brush top of dough lightly with olive oil. Place on baking sheet. Bake at 425° for 12 to 15 minutes, or until golden brown. Allow to cool. Place each in separate bag or wrap in plastic. Place wrapped calzones in gallon freezer bag. Label and freeze. 4 servings.

To serve: Heat in microwave. For crisper crust, broil for 1 to 2 minutes or heat in toaster oven.

 Calzones may be frozen prior to baking.

Turkey, Bacon and Cheese Pies

2 cups flour
1 tablespoon sugar
1 tablespoon salt
3/4 cup shortening
1 egg
1/2 cup cold water
1 tablespoon white vinegar
1 pound turkey tenderloin, cooked and shredded
1/2 pound bacon, cooked and torn
2 cups shredded Cheddar cheese
1 cup shredded Monterey Jack cheese
1 egg
1 teaspoon milk

Combine flour, sugar and salt. Cut in shortening until mixture is crumbly. Whisk together egg, water and vinegar. Stir in enough to moisten all the flour. Pat dough into a smooth, thick, flat disc. Wrap in waxed paper and refrigerate for at least one hour. On a lightly floured surface, roll out dough to 1/8-inch thickness. Using a 6-inch saucer as a guide, cut dough into 10 circles. Gather scraps and re-roll dough as necessary. Divide shredded turkey, bacon, Cheddar cheese and Monterey Jack cheese among the 10 circles. In a small bowl, beat egg with milk to make a glaze. Brush edges of dough with egg glaze and fold dough in half. Press edges together with a fork to seal. Pierce top of dough with a fork. Lightly brush pies with egg glaze. Bake at 400° for 15 to 20 minutes. Allow to cool. Place in freezer bag. Label and freeze. 10 servings.

To serve: Heat in microwave. For crisper crust, broil for 1 to 2 minutes or heat in toaster oven.

 Pies may be frozen prior to baking.

Chicken Taco Pizza

1 (16-ounce) can large refrigerated biscuit dough
1 cup cooked, chopped chicken
1/2 cup **Chunky Salsa** (page 286)
2 tablespoons **Taco Seasoning** (page 288)
2 green onions, sliced
1/2 cup sliced green bell pepper
1 1/2 cups shredded Cheddar cheese

Separate dough into 8 biscuits. Place on ungreased baking sheets and roll each biscuit to form a 5-inch round. Combine chicken, salsa and taco seasoning. Mix well. Spread about 1/3 cup chicken mixture on each round. Top with onions, bell pepper and cheese. Bake at 350° for 22 to 24 minutes. Allow to cool completely. Place each pizza in quart freezer bag. Label and freeze. 8 servings.

To serve: Heat in microwave or in toaster oven.

Crescent Wrapped Fish

1 (8-ounce) can refrigerated crescent roll dough
8 frozen breaded fish sticks
Tartar Sauce (page 282)
1 tablespoon melted butter

Separate dough into 8 triangles. Place 1 fish stick on shortest side of triangle. Spoon 1 heaping teaspoon of **Tartar Sauce** onto each fish stick. Roll up, starting with shortest side of triangle. Fish sticks will not be completely covered. Place rolled fish, point side down, on ungreased baking sheet. Brush each with melted butter. Bake at 375° for 12 minutes or until golden brown. Allow to cool. Place in single layer in gallon freezer bag. Label and freeze. 8 servings.

To serve: Heat in microwave or toaster oven. Serve with additional **Tartar Sauce.**

Tuna Triangles

2 (6-ounce) cans tuna, drained
1 cup shredded Cheddar cheese
2 tablespoons **Ranch Dressing** (page 263)
1 (8-ounce) cans refrigerated crescent roll dough

Combine tuna, cheese and dressing. Separate crescent roll dough into four rectangles. On an ungreased baking sheet, press each rectangle to 4 x 8 inches. Cut each rectangle in half to form eight squares. Mound tuna mixture on a diagonal half of each square, leaving a 1/2-inch border all around. Fold dough squares in half to form triangles. Press edges with a fork to seal. Cut a small slit in the top. Bake at 375° for 14 to 16 minutes or until golden brown. Allow to cool. Place in single layer in gallon freezer bag. Label and freeze. 8 triangles.

To serve: Thaw and heat in microwave. For crisper crust heat in toaster oven. Serve with **Ranch Dressing**.

Lime Coconut Shrimp

1/4 cup flour
2 tablespoons packed brown sugar
1/4 teaspoon salt
1 egg
1 tablespoon lime juice
1 cup sweetened flaked coconut
1 pound uncooked, peeled shrimp (about 40)
2 tablespoons melted butter

Combine flour, brown sugar and salt. In separate bowl, beat egg and lime juice. Place coconut in third shallow bowl. Coat each shrimp with flour mixture. Dip each into egg mixture. Coat well with coconut. Place on rack in broiler pan. Drizzle with melted butter. Bake 7 to 8 minutes until shrimp are pink and coconut is beginning to brown. Allow to cool. Place in gallon freezer bag. Label and freeze. 8 servings.

To serve: Microwave briefly, just until hot. Do not over cook. Serve with **Apricot Sauce** (page 274).

Shrimp may be frozen prior to baking. Place in single layer on baking sheet. Freeze until firm. Transfer to freezer bag. Label and freeze.

Assemble Recipes

Perfect Burgers

2 pounds lean ground beef
1/2 cup oatmeal
1/2 cup chopped onion
1 tablespoon minced green bell pepper
1/4 cup milk
1/4 cup ketchup
1 egg
1 teaspoon salt
1/8 teaspoon pepper

Combine ground beef, oatmeal, onion, green pepper, milk, ketchup, egg, salt and pepper. Shape into 8 patties. Arrange in a gallon freezer bag with waxed paper between each burger. Label and freeze. 8 servings.

To serve: Grill or broil until cooked through. Serve on toasted hamburger buns spread with **Simple Thousand Island Dressing** (page 269). Top with all the trimmings.

These burgers may be grilled, broiled or fried before freezing. Avoid overcooking. Freeze cooked burgers in individual bags for one or more quick servings.

Mushroom Bacon Burgers

4 slices bacon
2 tablespoons butter
1/2 cup sliced mushrooms
1 pound lean ground beef
2 tablespoons minced onion
1 1/2 teaspoons Worcestershire sauce
1 teaspoon soy sauce
1/2 teaspoon salt
1/4 teaspoon pepper

Cook bacon until crisp. Crumble and set aside. Melt butter in small skillet. Add mushrooms. Cook and stir until soft, lightly browned and the liquid has cooked away. Allow to cool. Combine cooled mushrooms, ground beef, crumbled bacon, minced onion, Worcestershire sauce, soy sauce, salt and pepper. Shape into 4 patties. Arrange in a gallon freezer bag with waxed paper between each burger. Label and freeze. 4 servings.

To serve: Grill or broil until cooked through. Serve on toasted hamburger buns with lettuce and tomato.

These burgers may be grilled, broiled or fried before freezing. Avoid overcooking. Freeze cooked burgers in individual bags for one or more quick servings.

Hoisin Garlic Burgers

1 pound lean ground beef
1/4 cup fresh bread crumbs
1/4 cup chopped green onion
2 tablespoons hoisin sauce
2 teaspoons minced garlic
1 teaspoon minced ginger
1 egg

In a bowl combine beef, bread crumbs, green onions, hoisin sauce, garlic, ginger and egg. Mix well. Shape into 4 patties. Arrange in a gallon freezer bag with waxed paper between each burger. Label and freeze. 4 servings.

To serve: In a small bowl, whisk together 2 tablespoons water, 2 tablespoons hoisin sauce and 1 teaspoon sesame oil. Brush half of the sauce over top of the burgers. Place on a greased grill or on the a rack on a baking sheet. Bake at 375° for 8 minutes. Turn patties once and brush with remaining sauce. Grill or bake for 8 more minutes. Serve on buns. Top with lettuce and tomato.

 To make fresh bread crumbs, place one slice of bread in a food processor. Pulse a few times until uniform crumbs form.

Hoisin sauce is found in the Oriental section of most grocery stores.

Jack Bacon Burgers

1 1/2 pounds lean ground beef
1/2 teaspoon onion salt
1/4 teaspoon pepper
6 thin slices Monterey Jack cheese
6 slices bacon

Form beef into 12 thin patties. Sprinkle with onion salt and pepper. Top each of 6 patties with a cheese slice. Top with another patty. Pinch edges to seal cheese inside. Wrap bacon slice around edge of each burger. Secure with a toothpick. Arrange in a gallon freezer bag with waxed paper between each burger. Label and freeze. 6 servings.

To serve: Thaw. Grill, broil or fry until cooked through. Remove toothpicks. Serve alone or on buns with lettuce and tomato.

 For spicier burgers substitute Pepper Jack cheese for the Monterey Jack cheese.

These burgers may be grilled, broiled or fried before freezing. Avoid overcooking. Remove toothpicks. Freeze cooked burgers in individual bags for one or more quick servings.

Teriyaki Burgers

1/4 cup soy sauce
1/4 cup sugar
2 teaspoons red wine vinegar
1 teaspoon sesame oil
1/2 teaspoon minced garlic
1/4 teaspoon ground ginger
1 1/2 pounds lean ground beef

In medium bowl, combine soy sauce, sugar, vinegar, oil, garlic and ginger. Mix until sugar is dissolved. Add ground beef. Mix with hands until completely mixed. Shape into 6 patties. Arrange in a gallon freezer bag with waxed paper between each burger. Label and freeze. 6 servings.

To serve: Grill or broil until cooked through. Serve on toasted hamburger buns with grilled pineapple rings and lettuce. Drizzle with **Sweet Onion Sauce** (page 278).

These burgers may be grilled, broiled or fried before freezing. Avoid overcooking. Freeze cooked burgers in individual bags for one or more quick servings.

Club Soda Burgers

1/2 pound lean ground beef
1/2 pound ground pork
1/2 cup chopped onion
1 egg
1/4 cup flour
3/4 teaspoon salt
1/4 teaspoon pepper
1/2 cup club soda

Combine ground beef and ground pork. Add onion, egg, flour, salt, pepper and club soda. Mix well. Place in freezer for 30 minutes, until mixture is chilled and easier to handle. Shape into 4 patties. Arrange in a gallon freezer bag with waxed paper between each burger. Label and freeze. 4 servings.

To serve: Heat 1 tablespoon oil and 1 tablespoon butter in skillet. Add burgers to skillet and simmer until cooked through. Serve on toasted hamburger buns with sweet onion slices and lettuce.

These burgers may be cooked before freezing. Avoid overcooking. Freeze cooked burgers in individual bags for one or more quick servings.

Meatloaf Burgers

1 pound lean ground beef
1/2 pound ground pork
1/2 cup fresh bread crumbs
1/2 cup ketchup
1/4 cup minced onion
1 egg
2 tablespoons Worcestershire sauce
1/2 teaspoon salt
1/4 teaspoon pepper

In a medium bowl, combine ground beef and ground pork. In a separate bowl, combine bread crumbs, ketchup, onion, egg, Worcestershire sauce, salt and pepper. Pour over combined meats. Mix gently to combine. Form into 6 patties. Arrange in a gallon freezer bag with waxed paper between each burger. Label and freeze. 6 servings.

To serve: Grill or broil until cooked through. Serve on toasted hamburger buns with crisp bacon and shredded lettuce.

These burgers may be grilled, broiled or fried before freezing. Avoid overcooking. Freeze cooked burgers in individual bags for one or more quick servings.

To make fresh bread crumbs, place one slice of bread into a food processor. Pulse a few times to make perfect crumbs.

Green Chile Burgers

2 pounds lean ground beef
3/4 cup **Chunky Salsa** (page 286)
2 eggs
1 (1.25-ounce) envelope taco seasoning

Combine ground beef, salsa, eggs and taco seasoning. Form into 10 patties. Arrange in a gallon freezer bag with waxed paper between each burger. Label and freeze. 8 servings.

To serve: Grill or broil until cooked through. Serve on toasted hamburger buns with **Green Chile Mayonnaise** (page 283) and **Chunky Salsa.**

These burgers may be grilled, broiled or fried before freezing. Avoid overcooking. Freeze cooked burgers in individual bags for one or more quick servings.

Pizza Burgers

1 pound lean ground beef
1/2 pound sweet Italian sausage
2 tablespoons spaghetti sauce
1 teaspoon Italian seasoning
1 (2.25-ounce) can sliced black olives
3/4 teaspoon salt
1/4 teaspoon pepper

Combine ground beef and sweet Italian sausage. Add spaghetti sauce, Italian seasoning, drained black olives, salt and pepper. Mix gently until well combined. Shape into 6 square patties. Arrange in a gallon freezer bag with waxed paper between each burger. Label and freeze. 6 servings.

To serve: Grill or broil until cooked through. Serve on thick slices of toasted French bread, with warmed spaghetti sauce, lettuce and sliced Mozzarella cheese.

These burgers may be grilled, broiled or fried before freezing. Avoid overcooking. Freeze cooked burgers in individual bags for one or more quick servings.

Chicken Fajita Burgers

1 tablespoon canola oil
1/4 cup chopped onion
1/4 cup chopped red bell pepper
1/4 cup chopped green bell pepper
1 teaspoon minced garlic
1 1/4 pounds ground chicken
1 tablespoon lime juice
1 teaspoon chili powder
1 teaspoon salt

Heat oil in large skillet. Add onions, red pepper and green pepper. Cook and stir until soft and lightly browned. Add garlic and cook for about 1 minute longer. Remove from heat. In a medium bowl, combine cooked vegetables, ground chicken, lime juice, chili powder and salt. Mix well. Using wet hands, shape into 6 oblong patties, about 2 x 4 inches. Arrange in a gallon freezer bag with waxed paper between each burger. Label and freeze. 6 servings.

To serve: Grill or broil until cooked through. Serve wrapped in warm tortillas with salsa and **Avocado Dressing** (page 272).

These burgers may be grilled, broiled or fried before freezing. Avoid overcooking. Freeze cooked burgers in individual bags for one or more quick servings.

Honey Mustard Turkey Burgers

1 1/2 pounds ground turkey
1 tablespoon minced onion
2 tablespoons honey
2 tablespoons mustard
1 teaspoon Worcestershire sauce
1 teaspoon salt
1/4 teaspoon pepper

Combine ground turkey with onion, honey, mustard, Worcestershire sauce, salt and pepper. Using wet hands, shape into 4 rectangular patties. Arrange in a gallon freezer bag with waxed paper between each burger. Label and freeze. 4 servings.

To serve: Grill or broil until cooked through. Serve on toasted French rolls with **Honey Mustard Dressing** (page 266), onion rings and lettuce.

For delicious variety, substitute other mustards such as Dijon or Spicy Brown mustard for the regular mustard.

These burgers may be grilled, broiled or fried before freezing. Avoid overcooking. Freeze cooked burgers in individual bags for one or more quick servings.

BBQ Turkey Burgers

1 1/4 pounds ground turkey
2 tablespoons chili sauce
1/2 cup chopped onion
1 teaspoon garlic salt
1/4 teaspoon pepper
2 tablespoon canola oil
1/2 cup chopped onion
3/4 cup chili sauce
1 tablespoon packed brown sugar
1 tablespoon mustard
1 tablespoon apple cider vinegar
2 teaspoons Worcestershire sauce
2 tablespoons water

Combine ground turkey, chili sauce, chopped onion, garlic salt and pepper. Using wet hands, form into 4 patties. Heat oil in large skillet. Add burgers and cook over medium heat until bottoms are browned, about 2 minutes. Turn burgers and sprinkle remaining onion around burgers. Cook, stirring onions occasionally, until burgers are browned and onions are soft, about 3 minutes. Add chili sauce, brown sugar, mustard, vinegar, Worcestershire sauce and water. Bring to a simmer and reduce heat. Cover and cook until burgers are cooked through and sauce is thickened, about 15 minutes. Allow to cool completely. Place carefully in single layer in freezer bag. Label and freeze. 4 servings.

To serve: Thaw and heat. Serve in pocket bread topped with shredded lettuce, diced tomato and shredded Monterey Jack cheese.

Salsa Turkey Burgers

1 1/4 pounds ground turkey
1 cup **Chunky Salsa** (page 286)
1/4 cup chopped onion
1 tablespoon chopped cilantro
1/2 teaspoon salt
1/4 teaspoon pepper

Combine ground turkey, salsa, onion, cilantro, salt and pepper. Shape into 4 patties. Arrange in a gallon freezer bag with waxed paper between each burger. Label and freeze. 4 servings.

To serve: Grill or broil until cooked through. Serve on toasted hamburger buns with avocado slices, shredded Cheddar cheese and shredded lettuce.

These burgers may be grilled, broiled or fried before freezing. Avoid overcooking. Freeze cooked burgers in individual bags for one or more quick servings.

Thanksgiving Burgers

2 tablespoons butter
1/4 cup chopped onion
1/4 cup chopped celery
1/3 cup chicken broth
3/4 cup seasoned stuffing mix
3/4 teaspoon salt
1/2 teaspoon poultry seasoning
1/4 teaspoon pepper
1 1/2 pounds ground turkey

Melt butter in small skillet. Add onion and celery. Cook and stir over medium heat until softened. Add broth and bring to a boil. Remove from heat. Stir in stuffing, salt, poultry seasoning and pepper. Allow to cool completely. In large bowl, combine ground turkey with cooled stuffing mixture. Shape into 6 patties. Arrange in a gallon freezer bag with waxed paper between each burger. Label and freeze. 6 servings.

To serve: Grill or broil until cooked through. Serve on toasted onion rolls. Top with cranberry sauce.

These burgers may be grilled, broiled or fried before freezing. Avoid overcooking. Freeze cooked burgers in individual bags for one or more quick servings.

Italian Heroes

1 pound lean ground beef
1 pound hot Italian sausage
1 cup chopped onion
3/4 cup chopped green bell pepper
2 teaspoon minced garlic
1 cup spaghetti sauce
1 (2.25-ounce) can sliced black olives
1 teaspoon sugar
1 1/2 cups shredded Mozzarella cheese
1 loaf French bread

Brown ground beef and sausage with onion, bell pepper and garlic until meat is no longer pink. Remove from heat. Stir in spaghetti sauce, drained olives and sugar. Stir in cheese. Slice top off bread. Pull out soft inside, leaving a 1-inch thick shell. Spoon filling inside bread shell. Replace top of loaf. Wrap tightly in extra heavy foil. Label and freeze. 8 servings.

To serve: Thaw. Bake in 350° oven for 45 minutes. Cut into 8 slices.

To slice the loaf, first remove the top. Slice the filled loaf, then slice the top and replace the top pieces.

Pizza Sauce

1/4 pound lean ground beef
1/4 pound Italian sausage
1/2 cup chopped onion
1 teaspoon minced garlic
1/2 teaspoon salt
1 (26-ounce) jar spaghetti sauce
1 tablespoon packed brown sugar

Brown ground beef and sausage with onion, garlic and salt. Remove from heat. Stir in spaghetti sauce and sugar. Place in freezer bags or containers for use in recipes. About 6 cups.

To serve: Thaw and heat. Use to make pizza or serve over pasta.

 Pizza Sauce is perfect for **English Muffin Pizza** (page 237) and **French Bread Pizza** (page 238).

English Muffin Pizza

8 English muffins
2 cups spaghetti sauce
2 cups shredded Mozzarella cheese
1/2 cup sliced mushrooms
1 (2.25-ounce) can sliced black olives, drained
1/4 cup chopped onion
1/4 cup chopped green bell pepper

Split and toast English muffins. Spread about 2 table-spoons sauce over each toasted English muffin half. Sprinkle with cheese. Top with mushroom, olives, onion and bell pepper. Sprinkle with a little more cheese. Press down firmly. Place each mini pizza in a sandwich bag. Place in single layer on a baking sheet. Place in freezer just until frozen. Transfer wrapped pizzas to a gallon freezer bag. Label and freeze. 16 servings.

To serve: Broil pizzas 4 inches from heat until lightly browned or heat in toaster oven.

 Use **Pizza Sauce** (page 236) for the spaghetti sauce.

French Bread Pizza

2 cups spaghetti sauce
1 (3-ounce) package sliced pepperoni
2 cups shredded Mozzarella cheese
1 loaf French bread

Place sauce, pepperoni and Mozzarella cheese in separate pint freezer bags. Place all 3 bags into a gallon freezer bag. Label and freeze. 8 servings.

To serve: Cut loaf of bread in half. On each half spread half the sauce, half the cheese and half the pepperoni. Broil for about 5 minutes until cheese is bubbly and beginning to brown.

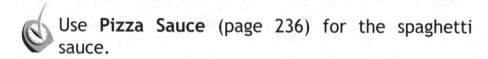

Use **Pizza Sauce** (page 236) for the spaghetti sauce.

French Bread may be frozen along with the pizza kit. Wrap the entire loaf tightly with extra heavy foil and freeze.

BBQ Chicken Mini Pizzas

6 English muffins
1 cup **BBQ Sauce** (page 280)
3 cups cooked, chopped chicken
1/4 cup chopped red onion
3 cups shredded Mozzarella cheese

Split and toast the English muffins. Spoon about 2 tablespoons BBQ sauce onto each half. Top with chopped chicken. Sprinkle with chopped red onion. Top with shredded cheese. Press down firmly. Place each mini pizza in a sandwich bag. Place in single layer on a baking sheet. Place in freezer just until frozen. Transfer wrapped pizzas to a gallon freezer bag. Label and freeze. 12 servings.

To serve: Broil pizzas 4 inches from heat until lightly browned or heat in toaster oven.

Double Crust Sloppy Joe Pizza

3 cups flour
3 cups instant mashed potatoes
2 cups milk
1/2 cup melted butter
1 pound lean ground beef
3/4 pound Italian sausage
1 cup chopped onion
1 (8-ounce) can tomato sauce
1 (6-ounce) can Italian tomato paste
2 tablespoons Sloppy Joe seasoning mix
    (from 1.25 ounce envelope)
1 (2.25-ounce) can sliced black olives
1 1/2 cup shredded Mozzarella cheese
1 tablespoon cornmeal

Stir together flour, dry potatoes, milk and melted butter. Set aside. In skillet, brown ground beef and sausage with chopped onion. Stir in tomato sauce, tomato paste, seasoning mix and drained olives. With floured hands, press half the dough into the bottom and about 1 1/2 inches up the sides of a 9 x 13 disposable foil baking pan. Spread filling over crust. Sprinkle with Mozzarella cheese. Place remaining dough between 2 sheets of waxed paper. Roll into a 15 x 11 inch rectangle. Remove top sheet and invert dough over filling. Remove paper. Trim edges as necessary. Turn edges of top crust under and seal to bottom crust. Sprinkle with cornmeal. Cover with extra heavy foil. Label and freeze. 8 servings.

To serve: Bake uncovered at 425° for 60 to 75 minutes or until heated through and crust is golden brown.

Beef Stuffed French Bread

1 loaf French bread
1 pound lean ground beef
1/4 cup chopped onion
1/4 cup chopped green bell pepper
1/4 cup chopped celery
1 (10.75-ounce) can Cheddar cheese soup
1 tablespoon Worcestershire sauce
1/2 teaspoon salt
pepper
4 slices American cheese

Slice the top off the bread. Pull out the soft center of the bread, leaving a 1-inch thick shell. Cut the removed bread into cubes. Brown ground beef with onion, green pepper and celery. Remove from heat. Stir in Cheddar cheese soup, Worcestershire sauce, salt and pepper. Mix well. Gently stir in bread cubes. Spoon into hollowed bread shell. Top with American cheese. Replace bread top. Wrap tightly with extra heavy foil. Label and freeze. 8 servings.

To serve: Thaw. Place foil wrapped bread on baking sheet. Bake at 350° for 30 minutes. Open foil down to pan. Return to oven for 15 minutes. Slice and serve. 6 servings.

To slice the loaf, first remove the top. Slice the filled loaf, then slice the top and replace the top pieces.

Stuffed Pizza Bread

1 pound mild Italian sausage
1 cup sliced mushroom
1/2 cup chopped onion
1 teaspoon minced garlic
1 (2-ounce) package sliced pepperoni
2 tablespoons tomato paste
1 teaspoon Italian seasoning
3/4 teaspoon salt
1/2 teaspoon sugar
1 cup shredded Mozzarella cheese
1 loaf frozen bread dough

Brown sausage with mushrooms, onion and garlic until meat is no longer pink. Remove from heat. Stir in pepperoni, tomato paste, Italian seasoning, salt and sugar. Cool completely. Stir in cheese. Thaw bread dough. Roll dough into a 10 x 14-inch rectangle. Spread cooled filling over dough, leaving a 1-inch border on all edges. Starting on long edge, roll up dough tightly. Pinch seams closed and fold short ends under roll. Wrap tightly with plastic. Place in gallon freezer bag. Label and freeze. 8 servings.

To serve: Thaw. Remove plastic. With a sharp knife, make three 1-inch slashes on top of loaf, cutting through to filling. Place on a greased baking sheet and brush lightly with olive oil. Bake at 400° for 35 to 45 minutes. Bread should be golden brown and sound hollow when tapped. Cool before slicing.

Beef Tacos

1 pound lean ground beef
1/4 cup flour
1 tablespoon chili powder
1/2 teaspoon salt
1/2 teaspoon garlic salt
1/2 teaspoon minced dried onion
1/4 teaspoon onion powder
1/2 teaspoon paprika
1/2 cup water

In a bowl, combine ground beef, flour, chili powder, salt, garlic salt, minced dried onion, onion powder and paprika. Using your hands, mix thoroughly. Heat the water in a large skillet. Add the ground beef mixture to the water. Cook over medium heat, stirring often to break meat into very small pieces. Allow to cool completely. Place in freezer bag or container. For individual servings, spray a muffin tin with non-stick cooking spray. Place about 3 tablespoons into each cup. Press down gently. Cover and freeze. When frozen, pop out and place in a gallon freezer bag. Label and freeze. 10 servings.

To serve: Thaw and heat. Spoon into warm taco shells. Top each with shredded lettuce, cheese and **Taco Sauce** (page 287).

 Beef Taco filling is perfect for **Beef Taco Salad** (page 244), **Beef Tostadas** (page 245) and **Beef Burritos** (page 247).

 To warm taco shells, place in a single layer on a baking sheet. Place in 400° oven for 5 minutes.

Beef Taco Salad

1 recipe **Beef Tacos** (page 243)
8 cups torn or shredded lettuce
4 cups broken tortilla chips
2 cups shredded Cheddar cheese
1 (2.25-ounce) can sliced black olives, drained
1/2 cup diced tomato
1 cup **Catalina Dressing** (page 265)
1 cup **Chunky Salsa** (page 286)

Prepare **Beef Taco** filling as directed. Allow to cool completely. Place in freezer bag or container. To freeze filling for individual salad servings, spray cups of a muffin tin with non-stick cooking spray. Fill cups with filling. Press down gently. Cover and freeze. When frozen, pop out and place in a gallon freezer bag. Label and freeze. 6 servings.

To serve: In large salad bowl (or in individual bowls) arrange lettuce and tortilla chips. Heat **Beef Taco** filling on stove top or in glass dish in microwave and add to salad. Top with cheese, olives and tomato. In small bowl combine **Catalina Dressing** and **Chunky Salsa**. Pour over salad and mix well.

Beef Tostadas

1 recipe **Beef Tacos** (page 243)
8 corn tostada shells
1 (16-ounce) can refried beans
1/4 cup water
2 cups shredded lettuce
1 cup shredded Cheddar cheese
Chunky Salsa (page 286)

Prepare **Beef Taco** filling as directed. Allow to cool completely. Place in freezer bag or container. For individual servings, spray a muffin tin with non-stick cooking spray. Place about 3 tablespoons into each cup. Press down gently. Cover and freeze. When frozen, pop out and place in a gallon freezer bag. Label and freeze. 8 servings.

To serve: In a small saucepan, heat refried beans and water. Cook and stir until smooth and creamy. Thaw and heat **Beef Taco** filling. Spread each warm tostada shell refried beans. Top with **Beef Taco** filling, then lettuce and cheese. Serve with **Chunky Salsa**.

 To warm tostada shells, place in a single layer on a baking sheet. Place in 400° oven for 5 minutes.

To make tostada shells from fresh corn tortillas, cook tortillas, one at a time in hot oil. Cook, turning once, until tortillas are golden brown and crispy. Be careful not to scorch tortillas.

Tomato Beef Tacos

1 pound lean ground beef
3/4 cup chopped onion
2 teaspoons minced garlic
1/8 teaspoon cayenne pepper
2 tablespoons chili powder
1/2 teaspoon cumin
3/4 teaspoon salt
1/2 teaspoon sugar
1 (8-ounce) can tomato sauce

Brown ground beef with onion and garlic until beef is no longer pink. Stir in cayenne pepper, chili powder, cumin, salt, and sugar. Cook and mix well. Stir in tomato sauce and cook until thickened, about 5 minutes. Allow to cool completely. Place in freezer bag or container. For individual servings, spray a muffin tin with non-stick cooking spray. Place about 3 tablespoons into each cup. Press down gently. Cover and freeze. When frozen, pop out and place in a gallon freezer bag. Label and freeze. 10 servings.

To serve: Thaw and heat filling. Spoon into warm taco shells or tortillas. Top each with shredded lettuce, sour cream and guacamole.

Use **Tomato Beef Tacos** for **Taco Salad** (page 248), **Beef Burritos** (page 247) and **Beef and Cheddar Quesadillas** (page 250).

Beef Burritos

1 recipe **Tomato Beef Tacos** (page 246)
8 flour tortillas
1 (16-ounce) can refried beans
1/4 cup water
2 cups shredded lettuce
1 cup shredded Monterey Jack cheese
1 cup shredded Cheddar cheese
1 cup sour cream
1 large avocado, diced
1/2 cup chopped onion
1/2 cup chopped tomato
Taco Sauce (page 287)

Prepare **Tomato Beef Taco** filling as directed. Allow to cool completely. Place in freezer bag or container. For individual servings, spray a muffin tin with non-stick cooking spray. Place about 3 tablespoons into each cup. Press down gently. Cover and freeze. When frozen, pop out and place in a gallon freezer bag. Label and freeze. 10 servings.

To serve: In small saucepan, heat refried beans and water. Cook and stir until smooth and creamy. Thaw and heat taco filling. For each burrito, spoon about 3 tablespoons refried beans down center of warm tortilla. Spoon about 3 tablespoons taco filling on top of beans. Top with lettuce, cheeses, sour cream, avocado, onion, tomato and **Taco Sauce**. Fold bottom and top edges of tortilla over filling. Fold one side over filling and roll up.

To heat tortillas, wrap in foil and bake in 425° oven for 10 to 15 minutes or place tortillas between damp paper towels and microwave on high for about 2 minutes. To heat one flour tortilla at a time, heat in microwave for about 15 seconds.

Taco Salad

1 recipe of **Tomato Beef Tacos** (page 246)
6 tortilla bowls
8 cups shredded lettuce
3 cups shredded Cheddar cheese
1 cup chopped tomato
Ranch Dressing (page 263)

Prepare **Tomato Beef Taco** filling as directed. Allow to cool completely. Place in freezer bag or container. To freeze filling for individual salad servings, spray a muffin tin with non-stick cooking spray. Fill cups with filling. Press down gently. Cover and freeze. When frozen, pop out and place in a gallon freezer bag. Label and freeze. 6 servings.

To serve: Thaw and heat filling. Fill tortilla bowls with lettuce, cheese, and tomato. Place heated taco filling on top. Serve with **Ranch Dressing**.

 Old Fashioned Chili (page 161) also makes great **Taco Salad.**

To make tortilla bowls, heat one 10-inch flour tortilla for 15 seconds in microwave. Gently press tortilla into a glass bowl, allowing sides to form rounded folds. Pierce bottom and sides of tortilla with a fork in 4 or 5 places to allow steam to escape and prevent bubbles. Place a glass custard cup or other small bowl in center of tortilla. Microwave for 1 minute. Pierce any bubbles with a fork. Microwave for about 1 minute longer, until edges are crispy and dry.

Cheesy Taco Salad

1 1/2 pounds lean ground beef
1 cup chopped onion
1 cup chopped celery
1 cup chopped green bell pepper
2 teaspoons minced garlic
1 pound loaf processed American cheese
1 (10-ounce) can diced tomatoes and green chiles
1 teaspoon sugar
2 teaspoon chili powder
2 teaspoons cumin

Brown ground beef with onion, celery, bell pepper and garlic. Cut cheese into cubes. Stir in cubed cheese, undrained tomatoes, sugar, chili powder and cumin. Cook and stir until cheese is melted. Allow to cool completely. Place in freezer bag or container. To freeze filling for individual salad servings, spray a muffin tin with non-stick cooking spray. Fill cups with filling. Press down gently. Cover and freeze. When frozen, pop out and place in a gallon freezer bag. Label and freeze. 8 servings.

To serve: Thaw and heat. Serve over shredded lettuce and crushed corn chips. Top with chopped green onion and tomatoes.

Beef and Cheddar Quesadillas

1 recipe **Tomato Beef Tacos** (page 246)
10 (8-inch) flour tortillas
2 tablespoons canola oil
2 cups shredded Cheddar cheese

Prepare **Tomato Beef Tacos** as directed. Allow to cool completely. Place in freezer bag or container. For individual servings, spray a muffin tin with non-stick cooking spray. Fill cups with filling. Press down gently. Cover and freeze. When frozen, pop out and place in a gallon freezer bag. Label and freeze. 10 servings.

To serve: Thaw and heat filling. Lightly brush one tortilla with oil and place on baking sheet. Spread **Tomato Beef Taco** filling over tortilla. Sprinkle generously with Cheddar cheese. Brush another tortilla with oil. Place on top of filled tortilla. Repeat for remaining tortillas. Bake at 325° in a single layer on baking sheets for about 8 minutes, until cheese is melted and quesadillas are heated through. Using pizza cutter, cut each quesadilla in wedges. Serve with salsa and sour cream.

Southwest Potato Skins

1 pound ground beef
1/2 cup chopped onion
1 (1.25-ounce) envelope taco seasoning
3/4 cup water
1 (2.25-ounce) can sliced black olives
12 small baked potatoes
1 1/2 cups shredded Cheddar cheese

Brown ground beef with onion. Stir in taco seasoning and water. Simmer for about 5 minutes. Stir in drained black olives. Cut baked potatoes in half. Scoop out potatoes leaving a 1/2-inch shell. Fill shells with meat mixture. Top with shredded cheese and press down to hold cheese in place. Place in freezer in single layer on baking sheet. When frozen, transfer to a freezer bag. Label and freeze. 24 pieces.

To serve: Broil 4 inches from heat for 3 to 5 minutes, until heated through and cheese is melted. Top with dollop of sour cream. Serve with **Chunky Salsa** (page 286) and **Ranch Dressing** (page 263).

Fried Chicken Strips

2 1/2 cups crushed saltine crackers
1 teaspoon garlic salt
1/2 teaspoon paprika
1/4 teaspoon lemon pepper
1 egg
1 cup evaporated milk
1 1/2 pounds boneless skinless chicken breast
oil for deep-frying

Combine cracker crumbs, garlic salt, paprika and lemon pepper. In a separate bowl, whisk together egg and milk. Cut chicken into 1/2-inch strips. Dip chicken strips into egg then coat with crumbs. deep-fry in hot oil (375°) for 2 to 3 minutes on each side or until golden brown. Drain on paper towels and allow to cool completely. Place in freezer bag. Label and freeze. 6 servings.

To serve: Thaw and heat. For crisper chicken strips, heat in toaster oven.

Wonton

1/2 pound lean ground beef
1/2 pound ground pork
3 cups finely shredded cabbage
1/2 cup sliced green onion
1 tablespoon soy sauce
1/2 teaspoon ground ginger
1/2 teaspoon salt
1/4 teaspoon pepper
1/2 (16-ounce) package round wonton wraps
4 1/2 tablespoons peanut oil

Combine ground beef, ground pork, shredded cabbage, onion, soy sauce, ginger, salt and pepper. Place about 1 tablespoon filling onto each wonton skin. Wet sides with water and seal. Heat 3 tablespoons peanut oil in skillet or wok. Stand wonton in skillet and cook for 2 to 3 minutes to brown the underside. Do not turn. Add 1/2 cup water to wok or skillet and cover. Steam over high heat until almost all the water is gone. Remove cover and add 1 1/2 tablespoons peanut oil. Reduce heat and cook until all the liquid is gone. Allow to cool completely. Place in single layer on a baking sheet. Cover and place in freezer until completely frozen. Place frozen wonton in a gallon freezer bag. Label and freeze. 30 wonton.

To serve: Thaw and heat in microwave. For crisper wonton, heat in toaster oven or under broiler. Serve with **Marmalade Dipping Sauce** (page 277).

 Wonton may be frozen before or after cooking.

Cream Cheese Chicken Ring

1/2 cup frozen French cut green beans
1 (10.75-ounce) can cream of chicken soup
1/2 cup cream cheese
2 cups cooked, chopped chicken
1 cup shredded Monterey Jack cheese
2 (8-ounce) cans refrigerated crescent roll dough

In small saucepan, cook green beans in boiling water for 10 minutes. Drain. Combine chicken soup and cream cheese. Mixture will not be smooth. Add chicken, cheese and drained beans. Mix well and place in freezer bag. Label and freeze. 8 servings.

To serve: Thaw chicken and heat. Separate crescent roll dough into triangles. On baking sheet, arrange triangles overlapping in a circle with the points pointing out. Spoon hot chicken filling in a ring on the dough. Lift the points up and over the filling, tucking under the center of the ring. Bake at 350° for 25 minutes.

Green Chile Chicken Wheel

2 cups cooked, chopped chicken
1/2 cup sour cream
1/4 cup chopped onion
1 (4-ounce) can diced green chiles
2 eggs
1/2 teaspoon pepper
1 teaspoon salt
2 cups shredded Monterey Jack cheese
1 loaf frozen bread dough

Combine chicken, sour cream, onion and green chiles. Beat eggs and add to chicken mixture. Stir in pepper, salt and cheese. Mix well. Thaw bread dough. Cut in half. Roll one half into a 13-inch circle on a greased piece of extra heavy foil. Spoon filling onto dough leaving edge clean. Roll other half of dough into a 13-inch circle. Place over filling and press edges together with a fork. Prick with a fork. Cover tightly with extra heavy foil. Label and freeze on pan until firm. (Pan may be removed once Chicken Wheel is frozen solid.) 8 servings.

To serve: Thaw. Bake at 400° for 1 hour. Remove foil and brush with beaten egg. Return to oven and bake uncovered for 15 minutes. Cut in wedges and serve plain or with **Green Chile Sour Cream** (page 281) and **Chunky Salsa** (page 286).

Fiesta Chicken Pie

1 3/4 cups flour
1 teaspoon salt
2/3 cup shortening
5 tablespoons cold water
1 1/2 cups cooked, chopped chicken breast
1 tablespoon olive oil
2/3 cup sliced onion
1/4 cup sliced red bell pepper
1/4 cup sliced green bell pepper
1/4 cup sliced yellow bell pepper
4 teaspoons fajita seasoning (from a 1.4-ounce envelope)
4 slices Pepper Jack cheese
1/2 cup **Chunky Salsa** (page 287)
1 egg, beaten

Combine flour and salt. Cut in shortening until mixture is crumbly. Stir in enough water to moisten all the flour. Pat dough into a smooth, thick, flat disc. Wrap in waxed paper and refrigerate for at least one hour. Divide dough in half. On a lightly floured surface roll both halves into a large circles. Place one dough circle on a piece of extra heavy foil, on a baking sheet. Heat oil in a large skillet. Cook onion and bell peppers until tender but not browned. Add chicken and fajita seasoning. Mix well. Spoon chicken onto bottom crust to within 1 inch of edge all around. Arrange cheese on chicken. Top with salsa. Brush edge of crust with water. Place remaining dough circle over filling. Press edges firmly together with a fork. Brush top with beaten egg. Top with another piece of extra heavy foil, folding top and bottom together to seal tightly. Label and freeze. 4 servings.

To serve: Take off top foil. Bake at 425° for 35 to 45 minutes or until deep golden brown. Serve with sour cream and additional **Chunky Salsa**.

Corn Dogs

1 cup flour
1/2 cup corn meal
1 tablespoon baking powder
1 tablespoon sugar
1 teaspoon salt
1/2 teaspoon ground mustard
dash pepper
1 cup evaporated milk
1 egg
8 hot dogs
8 bamboo skewers

Combine flour, corn meal, baking powder, sugar, salt, ground mustard, and pepper. Mix well. Beat milk and egg together. Add to dry ingredients. Mix well. Pour batter into a tall glass. Thread hot dogs onto skewers. Dip each hot dog into the batter filled glass. Deep-fry at 375° for about 2 minutes. Allow to cool completely. Place in freezer bag. Label and freeze. 8 servings.

To serve: Heat in microwave.

 Don't have any bamboo skewers? Popsicle sticks work just as well.

Make Mini Corn Dogs by using little smokies miniature hot dogs. Use toothpicks in place of the bamboo skewers.

Onion Rings

2 large sweet onions (Walla Walla or Vidalia)
2 1/2 cups buttermilk
3 tablespoons milk
2 eggs
1 3/4 cups flour
1 teaspoon salt
1 teaspoon garlic salt
1 teaspoon sugar
2 teaspoons chili powder
1/2 teaspoon pepper
oil for deep-frying

Slice onions and separate into rings. Soak rings in buttermilk for 30 minutes. In separate bowl, whisk together milk and eggs. In a shallow dish, (such as a pie plate) combine flour, salt, garlic salt, sugar, chili powder and pepper. Drain onion rings. Dip first in egg mixture then coat with flour mixture. Heat oil to 375° in electric skillet or deep-fryer. Deep-fry onion rings for 1 to 1 1/2 minutes on each side or until golden brown. Drain on paper towels. Spread cooked onion rings in a single layer on a cookie sheet. Place in freezer. When rings are frozen transfer to a freezer bag. Label and freeze. 4 servings.

To serve: Heat in toaster oven and serve.

Onion Rings may be frozen before deep-frying. Arrange coated onion rings in a single layer on a baking sheet. Cover and place in freezer. When rings are frozen transfer to a freezer bag. Label and freeze. To serve: Deep-fry rings in 375° oil for about 2 minutes per side or until golden brown.

Bacon Wrapped Shrimp

16 slices bacon
16 large uncooked, peeled shrimp
4 slices Pepper Jack cheese
1 teaspoon salt
1 teaspoon paprika
1/8 teaspoon pepper
dash cayenne pepper
4 skewers

In a large skillet, cook bacon for about 3 minutes per side. Bacon should be undercooked. Remove bacon and drain on paper towels. Cut a slice into the back of the shrimp but do not cut all the way through, creating a pocket for the cheese. Cut each cheese slice into 4 pieces. Stuff 1/4 cheese slice into each of the shrimp. Wrap a cooled bacon slice around the shrimp, starting over the cheese, and continue around the shrimp. Slide the shrimp onto a skewer. Repeat with remaining shrimp, placing 4 bacon wrapped shrimp onto each skewer with the tails going in the same direction. In a small bowl, combine salt, paprika, pepper, and cayenne pepper. Sprinkle lightly over shrimp. Place in gallon freezer bag, being careful not to pierce bag. Label and freeze. 4 servings.

To serve: Thaw. Broil for 3 to 4 minutes per side, until bacon begins to brown and cheese begins to melt. Serve with **Cocktail Sauce** (page 279).

Shrimp may be broiled prior to freezing. Freeze in a single layer. To serve, be careful to not overcook when reheating.

Caribbean Shrimp

2 tablespoons sliced green onion
2 teaspoons minced garlic
2 teaspoons grated lime peel
1/4 cup lime juice
1 tablespoon soy sauce
1/4 teaspoon pepper
1/8 teaspoon crushed red pepper flakes
1 1/2 pound uncooked, peeled shrimp (about 60)

Combine green onion, garlic, lime peel, lime juice, soy sauce, pepper and red pepper flakes. Stir in shrimp. Place in gallon freezer bag. Label and freeze immediately. 6 servings.

To serve: Thaw. Bake as soon as thawed, uncovered at 400° for 7 to 8 minutes.

Shrimp may be baked prior to freezing. Allow to marinate in sauce for 30 minutes to 4 hours before baking. Freeze in a single layer. To serve, be careful to not overcook when reheating.

Caribbean Shrimp Salad

1 recipe **Caribbean Shrimp** (page 260)
12 cups curly leaf lettuce
1 (8-ounce) can pineapple tidbits
1 (8-ounce) can Mandarin orange segments
1 kiwi
square wonton wraps
Honey Lime Dressing (page 267)

Prepare **Caribbean Shrimp** as directed. Place in freezer bag or container. To freeze shrimp for individual salad servings, spray cups of a muffin tin with non-stick cooking spray. Fill cups with shrimp and marinade. Press down gently. Cover and freeze. When frozen, pop out and place in a gallon freezer bag. Label and freeze. 6 servings.

To serve: Arrange lettuce in a large salad bowl (or in individual bowls). Add drained pineapple tidbits and drained Mandarin orange segments to salad. Peel kiwi, quarter and slice. Add kiwi to salad. Thaw and immediately bake shrimp at 400° for 7 to 8 minutes. Stack several wonton wraps. Cut through entire stack at once into very thin strips. Deep-fry in hot oil until golden and crispy. Pile on top of salad. Serve with **Honey Lime Dressing**.

For a nifty way to peel a kiwi, cut off both ends of the kiwi. Slide a spoon just under the skin and carefully slide the spoon around the kiwi. The skin will come off all in one piece.

Dressing and Sauce Recipes

Ranch Dressing

1/2 cup milk
1 tablespoon apple cider vinegar
1 cup mayonnaise
1 teaspoon garlic salt
1 teaspoon Accent
1 teaspoon pepper
1 teaspoon sugar

In a medium bowl, combine milk and vinegar. Stir. Add mayonnaise and whisk until smooth. Add garlic salt, Accent, pepper and sugar. Whisk until smooth. Cover and refrigerate. Shake before serving. 1 1/2 cups.

 A favorite dressing for salads. Try it on:
Island Beef Salad (page 142)
Sesame Chicken Salad (page 209)
Taco Salad (page 248)

 A favorite dipping sauce. Try it with:
Oven chicken Nuggets (page 206)
Pizza Potatoes (page 145)

 A favorite sandwich spread. Try it on:
Ranch Chicken Sandwiches (page 119)
Jack Bacon Burgers (page 224)

Italian Dressing

1 cup olive oil
1/4 cup white wine vinegar
1/4 cup lemon juice
2 teaspoons minced garlic
1 teaspoon salt
2 teaspoons sugar
1/2 teaspoon ground mustard
1/2 teaspoon paprika
1/2 teaspoon onion salt
1/2 teaspoon dried oregano

In a small bowl, combine oil, vinegar, lemon juice and garlic. Whisk until well blended. Add salt, sugar, ground mustard, paprika, onion salt and oregano seasoning. Whisk until smooth. Cover and refrigerate. Shake before serving. 1 1/2 cups.

Delicious dressing for salad. Try it on **Italian Beef Salad** (page 69) or **Pizza Joe Salad** (page 137).

Especially delicious on sandwiches, such as **Italian Beef** (page 68) or **Roast Pork Hoagies** (page 105).

Catalina Dressing

1/2 cup sugar
1/4 cup apple cider vinegar
1 teaspoon salt
dash paprika
1/4 teaspoon chili powder
1/4 teaspoon celery seed
1/4 teaspoon ground mustard
1 teaspoon onion
1/3 cup ketchup
1/2 cup canola oil

In a medium bowl, whisk together sugar and vinegar until sugar is dissolved. Stir in salt, paprika, chili powder, celery seed and ground mustard. Press onion through garlic press. Add to bowl. Stir in ketchup and vegetable oil. Whisk until smooth. Cover and refrigerate. Chill at least 30 minutes and shake before serving. 1 1/2 cups.

 Use this delicious salad dressing to make **Catalina Buns** (page 77).

Mix equal parts **Catalina Dressing** and **Chunky Salsa** (page 286) for a perfect dressing for taco salad. Try it on **Beef Taco Salad** (page 244).

Honey Mustard Dressing

1/2 cup mayonnaise
1/4 cup honey
2 tablespoons mustard
1/4 cup milk

In a small bowl, combine mayonnaise, honey, mustard and milk. Whisk until smooth. Cover and refrigerate. Stir before serving. 1 cup.

 A great salad dressing for **BBQ Pork Salad** (page 109).

 A perfect dipping sauce for **Cajun Chicken Nuggets** (page 152).

Honey Lime Dressing

1/3 cup lime juice
1/2 teaspoon grated lime peel
1/3 cup honey
1/2 cup canola oil
1 teaspoon ground mustard
1/2 teaspoon salt
dash pepper

In a small bowl, combine lime juice, lime peel, honey and oil. Whisk until well blended. Add ground mustard, salt and pepper. Mix well. Cover and refrigerate. Shake before serving. 1 1/2 cups.

 A delicious dressing for **Caribbean Shrimp Salad** (page 261).

To easily juice a lime, heat lime in the microwave in a glass bowl until the lime bursts (about 1 minute). Immediately stop microwave and allow lime to cool enough to handle. Juice can then be squeezed easily from the hole made by the escaping steam.

Poppy Seed Dressing

1/2 cup apple cider vinegar
1/2 cup sugar
1 teaspoon poppy seeds
1 teaspoon onion salt
1/2 teaspoon ground mustard
1 teaspoon salt
1 cup canola oil

In a small bowl, combine vinegar and sugar. Whisk until smooth and sugar is dissolved. Add poppy seeds, onion salt, ground mustard and salt. Mix well. Add oil. Whisk until smooth and glossy. Cover and refrigerate. Best prepared at least 24 hours before serving. Shake before serving. 2 cups.

 Delicious on **Apple Roast Pork Salad** (page 111).

Simple Thousand Island Dressing

2 cups mayonnaise
1/2 cup ketchup
1/2 cup sweet pickle relish
2 tablespoons sugar

In a small bowl, combine mayonnaise and ketchup. Whisk until smooth and well mixed. Add pickle relish and sugar. Mix well. Wait about 5 minutes to allow the sugar to completely dissolve. Mix again. Cover and refrigerate. Best served chilled. Stir before serving. 3 cups.

 A wonderful salad dressing, as easy as it is delicious. Try it on **Reuben Salad** (page 107).

 Delicious spread on burgers, such as **Perfect Burgers** (page 221) or on sandwiches, such as **Corned Beef Melts** (page 71).

Bleu Cheese Dressing

1 cup mayonnaise
1/4 cup buttermilk
2 tablespoons crumbled bleu cheese
1/8 teaspoon pepper
1/8 teaspoon onion powder
1/8 teaspoon garlic powder

Combine mayonnaise, buttermilk, cheese, pepper, onion powder and garlic powder in a small bowl. Mix well by hand, until mostly smooth. Cover and refrigerate. Chill at least 30 minutes and stir before serving. 1 1/2 cups.

 A great dipping sauce for **Buffalo Chicken Strips** (page 192).

 A perfect dressing for **Buffalo Chicken Salad** (page 193).

Chinese Salad Dressing

1/2 cup mayonnaise
5 tablespoons rice vinegar
2 tablespoons sesame oil
2 tablespoons sugar
1 tablespoon soy sauce
1/4 teaspoon garlic powder

In a medium bowl, combine mayonnaise, vinegar, oil and sugar. Whisk until smooth and sugar is dissolved. Add soy sauce and garlic powder. Mix well. Cover and refrigerate. Best served chilled. Shake before serving. 1 cup.

 A wonderful dressing for **Chinese Pork Salad** (page 113).

Avocado Dressing

1 large avocado
1/2 cup sour cream
2 teaspoons lemon juice
1 tablespoon onion
1 tablespoon water
1/4 teaspoon salt
1/4 teaspoon cayenne pepper

Peel avocado and mash in a mixing bowl. Stir in sour cream and lemon juice. Press onion through garlic press. Stir into avocado mixture. Add water, salt and cayenne pepper. Mix well. Cover and refrigerate. 1 1/2 cups.

Great as a dressing for **Beef Fajitas Salad** (page 87) and delicious spread on **Chicken Fajita Burgers** (page 230).

To peel an avocado, using a sharp knife, cut avocado in half lengthwise, down to the seed. Gently twist and pull halves apart. Tap the seed with the edge of a knife and lift the seed out. Slide a spoon just under the thick skin to remove the avocado.

Sweet and Sour Sauce

1/4 cup peach preserves
1/4 cup apricot preserves
2 tablespoons corn syrup
5 teaspoons apple cider vinegar
1 1/2 teaspoons corn starch
1/2 teaspoon mustard
3/4 teaspoon soy sauce
1/4 teaspoon garlic salt
2 tablespoons water

Combine all ingredients except water in a blender or food processor. Process until smooth. Transfer mixture to a small saucepan. Stir in water. Bring mixture to a boil over medium heat. Simmer for 5 minutes, stirring often. Remove from heat. Allow to cool. Cover and refrigerate. 3/4 cup.

A fabulous dipping sauce for chicken, egg rolls and wonton. Try dipping **Chicken Nuggets** (page 150), **Chicken Spring Rolls** (page 158) and **Chinese Triangles** (page 205).

Apricot Sauce

3/4 cup apricot preserves
1 tablespoon lime juice
1/2 teaspoon ground mustard

In small saucepan, combine apricot preserves, lime juice and ground mustard. Cook and stir over low heat, just until preserves are melted. Cover and refrigerate. 3/4 cup.

 Delicious as a dipping sauce for **Coconut Shrimp** (page 219).

Apricot Mustard Sauce

1 (12-ounce) jar apricot preserves
3 tablespoons mustard
2 tablespoons prepared horseradish

Combine apricot preserves, mustard and horseradish in a glass bowl. Microwave on High for 1 minute or until heated through. Serve warm. Cover and refrigerate. 1 1/2 cups.

 A zippy dipping sauce perfect for egg rolls or chicken. Try it with **Breaded Chicken Nuggets** (page 151).

Substitute other mustards, such as Dijon, Honey or Spicy Brown for the plain mustard.

Green Chile Ranch Sauce

1 cup **Ranch Dressing** (page 263)
1 (4-ounce) can diced green chiles

In blender, combine **Ranch Dressing** and diced green chiles. Blend until smooth. Cover and refrigerate. 1 1/2 cups.

 A great salad dressing that doubles as a fabulous dipping sauce. Try dipping **Taco Wings** (page 127).

Marmalade Dipping Sauce

1/2 cup orange marmalade
2 tablespoons chili sauce
1 tablespoon apple cider vinegar
1/2 teaspoon ground mustard

In small bowl, combine marmalade, chili sauce, vinegar and ground mustard. Mix well. Cover and refrigerate. 3/4 cup.

Serve with chicken, wonton or egg rolls. Especially delicious with **Coconut Chicken Fingers** (page 211) and **Wonton** (page 253).

Sweet Onion Sauce

1 cup corn syrup
2 tablespoons onion
2 tablespoons red wine vinegar
1 tablespoon white vinegar
2 teaspoons packed brown sugar
1/2 teaspoon lemon juice
1/4 teaspoon poppy seeds
1/4 teaspoon garlic salt
dash pepper

Combine all ingredients in a small saucepan. Heat to a rapid boil, stirring constantly. Remove from heat. Allow to cool. Cover and refrigerate. Shake before serving. 1 1/2 cups.

 This fabulous sauce is amazing drizzled on **Teriyaki Burgers** (page 225).

 It's called a sauce but it makes a wonderful salad dressing. Serve it on **Teriyaki Beef Salad** (page 191).

Cocktail Sauce

3/4 cup ketchup
2 tablespoons tomato paste
1 tablespoon prepared horseradish
1/4 cup lemon juice
1 tablespoon sugar
dash cayenne pepper

In a small bowl, combine ketchup, tomato paste, horse-radish and lemon juice. Stir well. Add cayenne pepper to taste. Cover and refrigerate. 1 cup.

A classic sauce perfect for almost any type of shrimp. Serve it with **Bacon Wrapped Shrimp** (page 259).

BBQ Sauce

1 (6-ounce) tomato paste
3/4 cup corn syrup
1/2 cup apple cider vinegar
1/4 cup packed brown sugar
3 tablespoons molasses
1 teaspoon liquid smoke
1/2 teaspoon garlic salt
1/2 teaspoon onion salt
1/4 teaspoon pepper
1 cup water

In a saucepan, combine tomato paste, corn syrup, vinegar, brown sugar and molasses. Stir in liquid smoke, garlic salt, onion salt, pepper and water. Bring to a boil. Reduce heat and simmer for about 30 minutes or until mixture is thick. Cover and refrigerate. 1 1/2 cups.

Use this delicious, slightly sweet, smoky sauce in any recipe that calls for barbeque sauce. It is the perfect sauce for **BBQ Chicken Mini Pizzas** (page 239).

Green Chile Sour Cream

1 (4-ounce) can diced green chiles
1 cup sour cream

In a small bowl, stir undrained chiles into sour cream.
Cover and refrigerate. 1 1/2 cups.

 The perfect dip to serve with **Green Chile Chicken Wheel** (page 255).

 A simple dip for a cool contrast to spicy **Texas Tenders** (page 212).

Tartar Sauce

1 cup mayonnaise
1 tablespoon minced onion
1 tablespoon minced dill pickle

In a small bowl, combine mayonnaise, onion and dill pickle. cover and refrigerate. Best prepared at least 30 minutes before serving. Cover and refrigerate. 1 cup.

Delicious and simple tartar sauce. Perfect to serve with **Crescent Wrapped Fish** (page 217) and **Tuna Triangles** (page 218).

For a sweeter **Tartar Sauce**, substitute salad dressing (such as Miracle Whip) for the mayonnaise and minced sweet pickle for the dill pickle.

Green Chile Mayonnaise

1 (4-ounce) can diced green chiles
3/4 cup mayonnaise

Place green chiles and mayonnaise in blender. Pulse a few times, leaving most of the green chiles in chunks. For a smoother dip, pulse a few more times until mostly smooth. 1 cup.

 A great spread for **Green Chile Burgers** (page 228).

 For spicier mayonnaise, substitute 1 (4-ounce) can diced jalapeños for the diced green chiles.

Honey Mayonnaise

1/2 cup mayonnaise
1/2 cup honey

In a small bowl, mix together mayonnaise and honey.
Chill and serve. 1 cup.

 A sweet and simple dip for chicken nuggets. Try it
with **Sesame Chicken Nugget**s (page 208).

Maple Syrup

1 cup sugar
1 cup packed brown sugar
3/4 cup water
1/2 teaspoon maple flavoring
1/2 teaspoon vanilla

In a saucepan, combine sugar, brown sugar and water. Heat just to boiling. Remove from heat. Stir in maple flavoring and vanilla. Allow to cool. Store covered. Serve warm. 2 cups.

A delicious and simple substitute for the real thing. Perfect on pancakes but also use it in any recipe that calls for maple syrup, such as **Maple Teriyaki Chicken Sandwiches** (page 121) and **Maple Chicken Wings** (page 126).

Chunky Salsa

1 (10.75-ounce) can tomato puree
1 1/3 cups water
1/3 cup chopped onion
1/3 cup chopped green bell pepper
1 (4-ounce) can diced green chiles
2 tablespoons white vinegar
1/4 teaspoon pepper
1/4 teaspoon salt
1/4 teaspoon minced dried onion
1/4 teaspoon minced dried garlic
1 tablespoon sugar

Combine all ingredients in a saucepan. Bring to a boil. Reduce heat and simmer for 30 minutes or until thickened. Cover and refrigerate. 2 cups.

A thick, delicious salsa that is great in any recipe that calls for salsa. Try it on **Chicken Taco Pizza** (page 216), **Green Chile Burgers** (page 228), **Salsa Turkey Burgers** (page 233), **Beef Tostadas** (page 245) and **Southwest Potato Skins** (page 251).

Mix equal parts **Chunky Salsa** and **Catalina Dressing** (page 265) for a perfect dressing for taco salad. Try it on **Beef Taco Salad** (page 244).

Taco Sauce

3 cups water
2 teaspoons cornstarch
3 tablespoons white vinegar
1 (6-ounce) can tomato paste
2 teaspoons sugar
4 teaspoons chili powder
1 teaspoon garlic salt
1 teaspoon salt
1/4 teaspoon cayenne pepper
1/4 teaspoon pepper

In medium saucepan, combine water and cornstarch, stirring until dissolved. Whisk in vinegar, tomato paste, sugar, chili powder, garlic salt, salt, cayenne pepper and pepper. Bring to a boil over medium heat. When mixture boils, reduce heat and simmer for 5 minutes. Allow to cool. Cover and refrigerate. 3 cups.

A fabulous sauce for tacos, burritos and tostadas. Try it on **Beef Tacos** (page 243) and **Beef Burritos** (page 247).

Taco Seasoning

2 teaspoons chili powder
1 1/2 teaspoons minced dried onion
2 tablespoons flour
1 1/2 teaspoons garlic salt
3/4 teaspoon beef bouillon
1/2 teaspoon sugar
1/4 teaspoon onion powder
dash cayenne pepper

In a small bowl, combine chili powder, minced dried onion, flour, garlic salt, bouillon, sugar, onion powder and cayenne pepper. Mix well. 4 tablespoons.

 Use in **BBQ Pork Tacos** (page 92) and **Chicken Taco Pizza** (page 216).

 One recipe of **Taco Seasoning** can be used in place of one (1.25-ounce) envelope of taco seasoning.

Recipe Index